Britain by the Book

Also by Oliver Tearle

The Secret Library

Britain by the Book

A Curious Tour of
Our Literary Landscape

OLIVER TEARLE

JOHN MURRAY

First published in Great Britain in 2017 by John Murray (Publishers)
An Hachette UK Company

1

© Oliver Tearle 2017

A CIP catalogue record for this title is available from the British Library

ISBN 978-1-47366-601-6
Ebook ISBN 978-1-47366-602-3

Typeset in Bembo Book MT Std 12/15 pt by
Palimpsest Book Production Limited, Falkirk, Stirlingshire

Printed and bound in Great Britain by Clays Ltd, St Ives plc

John Murray policy is to use papers that are natural,
renewable and recyclable products and made from wood grown in sustainable
forests. The logging and manufacturing processes are expected to conform to the
environmental regulations of the country of origin.

John Murray (Publishers)
Carmelite House
50 Victoria Embankment
London EC4Y 0DZ

www.johnmurray.co.uk

Preface

Britain is teeming with interesting literary stories. Take just one road in central London, Wimpole Street in Marylebone. At number 50 lived a poet, Elizabeth Barrett, whose correspondence – and subsequent elopement – with fellow poet Robert Browning in the 1840s inspired a play, *The Barretts of Wimpole Street*. At number 67 we find the childhood home of Arthur Hallam, Tennyson's university friend whose sudden death in 1833 inspired his great poem *In Memoriam*; Tennyson referred to it as a 'dark house' in an 'unlovely street'. Up the road, at 2 Upper Wimpole Street, Sir Arthur Conan Doyle set up his ophthalmology surgery in 1891, not far from Baker Street where he would locate Sherlock Holmes's iconic home. (According to his autobiography, Conan Doyle never had a single patient while he was there; luckily, 1891 was also the year that the first hugely popular Sherlock Holmes short story appeared in the *Strand* magazine, so this didn't matter.) Wilkie Collins moved to number 82 Wimpole Street in 1888, a year before he died. And this is just Victorian literary history we're talking about, all found on one London street.

The more I've studied and written about English literature – which is my day job as a lecturer in English at Loughborough University – the more interested I've become in the curious ways in which the paths of writers have crossed in a particular town, or on a specific street, or even in the same house. Staying in London, for instance,

I was surprised to learn that Sylvia Plath took her life in a flat that W. B. Yeats had once lived in. On a slightly less gloomy note, it's nice to reflect that when a young George Orwell, who was then still plain old Eric Blair, attended Eton, one of his teachers was Aldous Huxley.

This book is a curious literary tour of Britain, taking in the colourful characters and surprising stories from the country's rich literary history. *Britain by the Book* covers the Northumbrian goatherd at Whitby Abbey who composed one of the first English poems, England's first modern biographer and his pioneering exploration of Stonehenge, and how the world's longest-running play had a rather muted premiere in Nottingham. The book considers the role of the British landscape in inspiring classic works of literature and the ways writers have used, and even helped to create, British landmarks.

The meandering journey that follows has a point, of sorts. Chiefly, of course, the aim is to go in search of the most interesting stories to be found on this most literary of isles, but there is another objective, in that I have endeavoured wherever possible to unearth the more surprising and lesser-known links between authors and locations. Are we right to associate Wordsworth and the Romantic movement so closely with the Lake District? What about the significant time Wordsworth and Coleridge spent in Somerset, where they wrote much of *Lyrical Ballads* and were investigated for spying? Conversely, in our rush to associate Stratford-upon-Avon with Shakespeare, we overlook the fact that other writers of note lived in that town – including the bestselling novelist of the late nineteenth century, a woman whose name is now hardly known.

Such acts of displacement are designed to question the

long-standing associations between writer and place and to examine the alternative lives led by writers, often in very different and surprising parts of the country. After all, one of the things that will soon emerge before we've got very far on our literary tour is that many authors known for writing about a particular place did so only after they had stopped living there. George Eliot wrote beautifully about the Midlands, but only once she had moved down to London and Surrey, where she took up tennis lessons. Sticking with Surrey and games, it was here that the first celebrity cricket team was formed by the creator of Peter Pan, J. M. Barrie – a Scotsman who embraced one of England's most popular sports more fervently than most Englishmen do. Such unusual associations are to be found all over our British landscape.

I'm also interested in the surprising connections between different writers or literary works in a particular location. For instance, to many readers Binsey in Oxfordshire will immediately suggest Gerard Manley Hopkins's poem 'Binsey Poplars', but this small village also has a very sweet link (and 'sweet' in more ways than one) to Lewis Carroll's *Alice's Adventures in Wonderland*. Indeed, sometimes the journey will be a bit of a zigzag rather than a straight line. But then, that's the beauty of a journey by book – a few bumpy roads won't inconvenience anyone.

This book is a distillation of a great deal of reading and research. I read a whole book on the history of Hay-on-Wye, and now know far more about that tiny town on the Welsh borders than I ever thought I'd need to. But first and foremost I'm indebted to the vast reference work that is *The Oxford Guide to Literary Britain and Ireland*, which contains a raft of information about the literary associations of towns, cities, and villages throughout the British Isles. (At the end of this book you'll find a selected bibliography containing some of the other books I've found particularly useful in the course of researching it.) What has made writing this book a continual joy is the number of things I discovered that I never knew before, but thought I did. So if, like me, you are confident you know which Dorset-based writer resurrected the term 'Wessex', or can name King Arthur's court, or know the original location of Robin Hood's forest, then read on and prepare to be surprised. I was. But then I'm surprised I've still got my own hair.

Oliver Tearle
Loughborough, 2017

The Disappearing 'Round Table' of John O'Groats

It is traditional to cycle from Land's End to John O'Groats. At least, it is if you're intending to travel from one end of Britain to the other; that sort of thing would probably get you disqualified from the Tour de France. But our bookish tour begins at John O'Groats and will meander down the country towards Land's End at the other . . . well, the other end.

And John O'Groats has been seen as the most northerly point of the British mainland for a while. This is odd, given that it's not: that title goes instead to Dunnet Head, a few miles west of John O'Groats and several miles north of it, no matter how you view it. John O'Groats isn't even the most north-easterly point of the country, with Duncansby Head snatching that honour. But John O'Groats *is* the most north-easterly settlement, and that's what matters, especially when you're attempting to traverse Britain from one end to the other and want to ensure you have a bed for the night and somewhere to get some bacon and eggs to eat after what is, let's face it, a pretty long bike ride.

The tiny village of John O'Groats is named after a Dutchman, Jan de Groot, who began operating a ferry service out to the Orkneys at the end of the fifteenth century. The story goes that members of the family ended up falling out, with de Groot's children squabbling over who would inherit the ferrying business when their father died; de Groot senior promptly built an eight-sided house containing an octagonal table, as a way of resolving this dispute and ensuring that none of his family members might be viewed as the 'favourite'. Like King Arthur's round table, this tale of octagonal furniture is probably nothing more than legend. But in any case, the John O' Groats House Hotel, which is still open for business, includes an octagonal tower as a tribute to de Groot's original dwelling.

People have been walking from Land's End to John O'Groats, and vice versa, since at least 1871, when two brothers named John and Robert Naylor decided to saunter all the way from Scotland's most north-easterly mainland settlement down to south-west Cornwall, going the entire way on foot, at the height of the railway boom. In 1916 they published a book recounting their journey, *From John O' Groat's to Land's End; Or, 1372 Miles on Foot*. They, too, had difficulty finding Jan de Groot's original house, though they found 'a few mounds of earth covered with grass', which were all that was left of the structure; it had apparently been dismantled in order to build a granary. While staying at the Huna Inn a few miles west of John O'Groats, the brothers were handed an 1839 book by the house's landlady. In it they learned they weren't the first tourists to be thwarted in their quest to find de Groot's house:

> I went in a boat
> To see John o' Groat,
> The place where his home doth lie;
> But when I got there,
> The hill was all bare,
> And the devil a stone saw I.

John O'Groats is iconic as the end – or the beginning – of a journey that crosses Britain from one side to the other. Yet in 2010, it received the dubious accolade of 'Scotland's most dismal town'. This is inaccurate for at least one reason, namely that John O'Groats is a village rather than a town (we'll come to the UK's smallest town later on). But then isn't its dismalness the point? It's the end of the earth – well, all right, the end of Britain – and its bleakness is part of its odd charm.

But look at it how you will, there isn't much going on this far north, so perhaps we should venture a little further south, to the lake where a Victorian poet became the victim of a rather cruel joke . . .

A Bad Poet at Loch Ericht

We begin in the Highlands of Scotland, on the shores of Loch Ericht, where the Victorian poet Arthur Hugh Clough and his friends Tom Arnold and John Campbell Shairp (a young Scotsman who would later be Professor of Poetry at Oxford) stayed in September 1847. Their visit to Loch Ericht inspired Clough's long narrative poem *The Bothie*.

Not everyone liked *The Bothie*. In some quarters it was condemned as 'indecent and profane, immoral and communistic'. And indeed Clough wasn't greatly liked by many of his contemporaries: Tennyson called him 'good man Dull', while Algernon Charles Swinburne, not one to mince his words, declared Clough 'a bad poet'. Now, Clough's poetry is not read much, aside from the anthology favourite 'Say Not the Struggle Naught Availeth'. But in 1848, *The Bothie* attracted a fair number of readers and quite a lot of attention.

Unfortunately, this would not be an entirely good thing. The full title of Clough's poem is *The Bothie of Toper-na-Fuosich*. What does it mean? A 'bothie' is a local word for a forester's hut, but what about the rest of it? Loch Ericht is sometimes assumed to be the location (though precisely where on the loch nobody knows) of Toper-na-Fuosich, which Clough namechecks in the title of his poem. But it was pointed out that the name of the location his poem mentions, Toper-na-Fuosich, is, as a reviewer in the *Literary*

Gazette observed, from 'an ancient Highland toast to the female genital organs'. The reviewer remarked, 'the author ought to have been more guarded against the malicious Gael who imposed it on the inquisitive Sassenach [English person]'. A Scottish local, it would seem, had been pulling Clough's leg.

When Clough discovered his error, he was mortified. In February 1849, he wrote to Tom Arnold, who had accompanied him on the highland camping trip but was now living in New Zealand: 'It is too ludicrous not to tell someone, but too appallingly awkward to tell anyone on this side of the globe: – in the Gath and Ascalon of the Antipodes you may talk of it, and laugh at your pleasure.' In 1855, he wrote to a friend about his poem: 'I was so disgusted with the mishap of the name, that I have never had pleasure in it since.' Clough quietly altered the title of his poem to the more innocent (if entirely nonsensical and made-up) *The Bothie of Tober-na-Vuolich* for further editions, but it didn't help. His great work was, in his head, tarnished forever.

He could have consoled himself that he was not the only Victorian poet to have made such an embarrassing error. Indeed, others had made distinctly more blush-inducing ones. Consider poor Robert Browning, whose dramatic work, *Pippa Passes* (1841), inadvertently contained a word you wouldn't expect to find gracing the lines of a Victorian poem: mistakenly thinking the word 'twats' referred to a nun's hat, Browning innocently used the word in his verse drama. When James Murray and the other early editors of the *Oxford English Dictionary* later approached Browning to enquire about the source of the poet's knowledge of this indelicate word, Browning directed them to the little-known 1660 poem *Vanity of Vanities*:

> They talk't of his having a Cardinalls Hat:
> They'd send him as soon an Old Nuns Twat.

None of Browning's friends appears to have been brave enough to point out his mistake.

The Bard of Dundee

Arthur Hugh Clough may have been a bad poet, as Swinburne asserted, but he was not the worst poet of the nineteenth century by any means. The poet who is widely regarded as the worst of all is so bad that he is, in fact, really quite good.

It was in Paton's Lane, Dundee, in June 1877 that a flash of poetic inspiration struck. The poet who experienced this lightbulb moment was William Topaz McGonagall, famed – if that is quite the word – as probably the worst poet in the English language. He was reportedly the inspiration for the name Professor McGonagall in J. K. Rowling's *Harry Potter* series. Rowling liked the idea that her brilliantly clever character might be a distant relative of such a buffoon.

And a buffoon he most certainly was. McGonagall was born in March 1825, though his own account of his date of birth varied from one telling to the next. Despite his reputation as a Scottish poet, he was actually born to Irish parents, though he spent much of his adult life in Dundee. When he resolved to become a poet, he wrote to Queen Victoria requesting her patronage. She sent back a polite rejection letter, which McGonagall – never one to be blighted by a lack of self-confidence – interpreted as an expression of interest. In July 1878, over the course of three days, he walked sixty miles from his home in Dundee to the Queen's castle at Balmoral, enduring violent thunderstorms and a night's sleep in a barn, in order to perform a reading of his poetry in front of her. He was refused entry and had to walk all the way home again.

Performance, it must be said, was in his blood. When he played Macbeth in an amateur production of the Scottish play, he refused to die at the end, deciding that a little revision of the Bard's great tragedy was required. He had persuaded a local theatre to let him take the title role in the production, but he was so annoyed by the actor playing Macduff, who he reckoned was trying to upstage him, that he resolved not to fall down at the end of the play, causing consternation to the audience – and to Macduff, one suspects.

McGonagall also enjoyed performing his own poetry. Later in life he had a job giving poetry readings in a circus: he received fifteen shillings a night on condition that the crowd be allowed to pelt him with eggs and rotten food, like a minor criminal in the stocks. Surprisingly, McGonagall seemed to like this arrangement – the money came in handy – and he was annoyed when the authorities put a stop to it.

None of this perturbed him. He'd written his first poem about a reverend, George Gilfillan, himself something of a poetaster who was active in the 'Spasmodic School' of poetry, characterised by intense psychological drama and long-winded self-absorbed soliloquies. When Gilfillan read 'An Address to the Rev. George Gilfillan', he commented that 'Shakespeare never wrote anything like this' – an assessment with which, upon reading McGonagall's poem, a reader can only wholeheartedly agree. But McGonagall got a real chance to flex his poetic muscles in December 1879, when the Tay Rail Bridge in Dundee collapsed, killing everyone aboard the train crossing the bridge, reckoned to be some seventy-five people. Soon after the event, in 1880, McGonagall – regrettably – took up his pen to write an elegy for the lost souls, whose number he raised to ninety. The intention, no doubt, was to create a moving elegy for the victims and to do for the Tay Bridge what the Poet Laureate, Tennyson, had done for the Charge of the Light Brigade. Unfortunately, McGonagall's cack-handed way with rhyme had quite the opposite effect. Here's how it opens:

> Beautiful railway bridge of the silv'ry Tay
> Alas! I am very sorry to say
> That ninety lives have been taken away
> On the last sabbath day of 1879
> Which will be remember'd for a very long time.

It ends with the resounding couplet: 'For the stronger we our houses do build, / The less chance we have of being killed.'

McGonagall revealed in his autobiography the precise moment he discovered his 'genius' for poetry:

Dame Fortune has been very kind to me by endowing me with the genius of poetry. I remember how I felt when I received the spirit of poetry. It was in the year of 1877, and in the month of June, when the flowers were in full bloom. Well, it being the holiday week in Dundee, I was sitting in my back room in Paton's Lane, Dundee, lamenting to myself because I couldn't get to the Highlands on holiday to see the beautiful scenery, when all of a sudden my body got inflamed, and instantly I was seized with a strong desire to write poetry, so strong, in fact, that in imagination I thought I heard a voice crying in my ears – 'Write! Write!'

Would that we were all so endowed. The titles of McGonagall's successive collections of verse – and there were a lot of them – say it all: *Poetic Gems*, *More Poetic Gems*, *Still More Poetic Gems*, *Yet More Poetic Gems*, *Further Poetic Gems*, *Yet Further Poetic Gems*, and, eventually, *Last Poetic Gems*.

It's not simply that McGonagall's poetry was bad. It was, as the phrase has it, so bad it's good. As Stephen Pile notes in his *Book of Heroic Failures*, 'He was so giftedly bad that he backed unwittingly into genius.' For all the wrong reasons, McGonagall had seized upon the right word to describe himself: he *was* a genius.

Futuristic Golf at St Andrews

A game of golf at St Andrews may not be an obvious subject for futuristic fiction, but in 1892 that didn't stop a Scottish golfer named J. McCullough from writing a utopian novel with the glorious title *Golf in the Year 2000; or, What Are We Coming To.*

The plot of the book is relatively simple. In March 1892, Alexander John Gibson falls asleep and wakes 108 years later in the brave new world of the year 2000. He then proceeds to explore this new world, though his ambitions don't appear to extend further than seeing how much the local golf course has altered in the intervening century. Nevertheless, the book accurately predicted many things, including television (in McCullough's novel, international golf matches are televised), high-speed bullet trains, digital watches, driverless golf carts, British decimal currency, and women's liberation, although McCullough's golf jackets that yell 'Fore!' whenever the golfer swings his club remain the stuff of science fiction (though more through lack of interest than scientific impossibility, I imagine), and we haven't yet developed hairbrushes that keep hair at whatever length the owner wishes, which is more of a shame. It has even been claimed that the international golf tournament depicted in the book foreshadows the Ryder Cup, which wasn't established for another thirty-five years.

But McCullough's novel is not a wholly serious utopian novel, unlike Edward Bellamy's bestselling *Looking*

Backward: 2000–1887, which had been published in the US four years earlier and had been hugely influential among socialist clubs and radical political groups. The book's preface proudly states, 'I began with the intention of having a moral, but I hadn't gone very far when I forgot what the moral was, so I left it out. Of course that's not to say that the book is immoral – far from it.' In many respects, McCullough's book is closer to Jerome K. Jerome's comic fiction and might even be described as a precursor to P. G. Wodehouse's golfing stories. Even the short chapter summaries compel you to read more:

> In a curious position – Discover I have grown a beard – Am nearly drowned – Mr. Adams, C.I.G.C. – The year 2000 – The certificate – Get my hair cut – The watch

If that whets your appetite for chapter one – as it should – you can read on to chapter seven, which treats the women of this future world:

> How they cross the Atlantic – What the ladies of 2000 do – Miss Adams – Has the female sex degenerated? – The picture gallery – Miss Adams again, a little too much of her this time

Women, who dress like men in McCullough's imagined future, have attained many of the top business roles because they can actually get things done, whereas the men, as the book's title implies, simply stand around and play golf.

As you'd expect from a book about golf written by a Scottish writer, *Golf in the Year 2000* features a trip to St Andrews, which, the narrator informs us, is 'not what it was in my day'. The course has been replanned and the time taken to traverse it has greatly increased, and the narrator becomes distinctly annoyed by the speaking jacket (the one that yells 'Fore!') which he is required, by club rules, to wear. So, more of a nightmare dystopian vision, then?

Ettrick, Scottish Borders

Let's leave St Andrews behind, but stick with the sports theme and go in search of the Scottish Olympics, which were the vision of one man, a writer whose name is not as celebrated as it should be.

For many years the Scottish author James Hogg thought he shared his birthday, 25 January, with Robert Burns, whom he believed to be thirteen years his senior. He was crestfallen to learn, later in life, that he'd been baptised over a year before he was (apparently) born – the parish register had his baptism recorded in December 1770, which would have made it difficult for him to have been born in January 1772, as he'd previously thought.

Hogg had, in fact, been born at the farm of Ettrick Hall in Selkirkshire, an area known for its sheep farming. His father had been wealthy but bankruptcy meant that young James had to scrape a living herding cattle on local farms. Having literally lost the shirt off his back, he was reduced to working topless – a sight that was rendered even more 'grotesque', in his own words, by the fact that he 'could never induce my trews, or lower vestments, to keep up to their proper sphere, there being no braces in those days'. Work among the fields of Selkirkshire must have been *very* exposing.

By the time he'd reached adulthood, Hogg had become a shepherd at the nearby Blackhouse Farm, and had ready access to a vast collection of books which he read his way through as if his life depended on it. It seems that everyone active on the literary scene at this time somehow knew each other, despite the relatively isolated nature of the rural communities in Scotland: Hogg came to know Burns's widow, Jean Armour, and was friends at Blackhouse with William Laidlaw, the man who would later manage Sir Walter Scott's estate at Abbotsford (of which more anon when we arrive there). Hogg and Scott became friends too, with the latter encouraging 'Jamie the Poeter', as he was becoming known, to publish the writing Hogg had been working on.

Indeed, it was Hogg's links with other writers of the day that led to one of the most bizarre literary anthologies Britain has ever seen. In 1816, in order to support his establishment at Eltrive Farm in Yarrow, Hogg decided to compile a collection of poems by other living poets. However, despite his friendship with writers like Scott, and initial interest in the project from many of the poets he wrote to, Hogg ultimately found his contemporaries reluctant to contribute. Wordsworth originally agreed, but then withdrew his poem. Scott, on whom Hogg thought he could rely to offer his support, refused point-blank because he lacked faith in the enterprise. Undeterred, Hogg simply sat down and wrote his fellow writers' poems for them, parodying their styles with relentless relish. The result was *The Poetic Mirror*, a collection of inspired parodies of the major poets of the age. Wordsworth features in 'The Flying Tailor' among others, while Coleridge is lampooned in 'Isabelle', a nod to his poem 'Christabel'.

The Poetic Mirror, and a string of novels – the most famous of which is *The Private Memoirs and Confessions of a Justified Sinner*, whose influence can be seen in Robert Louis

Stevenson's *Strange Case of Dr Jekyll and Mr Hyde* – established Hogg as a literary star, and, after Sir Walter Scott, the most famous Scottish writer of the time. At Innerleithen, some 18 miles north of Ettrick, Hogg founded the St Ronan's Border Games in the 1820s, featuring angling, archery, athletics, curling, rifle shooting, and wrestling, among other events. The games were named after Scott's 1824 novel *St Ronan's Well*, which was set in Innerleithen, and are sometimes known as the 'Scottish Olympics'. The entry on Hogg in the *Oxford Dictionary of National Biography* never even mentions the games or his role in establishing them. Some of his achievements, it would seem, are still little known or little appreciated.

Alloway, Ayrshire

Burns Night is known and celebrated throughout the world. Every 25 January – the day James Hogg wrongly considered to be his own birthday – millions of people toast Scotland's national poet, address the haggis, and read the poetry of Robert Burns.

The traditions of Burns Night can be traced back to 1801, when nine of Robert Burns's friends gathered in his cottage in Alloway to celebrate the poet on . . . well, on 21 July. This is because the very first Burns Night was held on the five-year anniversary of the poet's death.

That changed the following year when the oldest surviving Burns club (in Greenock) gathered to celebrate Burns on the anniversary of his birth, rather than death. Yet even they managed to get the date wrong. They laboured under the misapprehension that Burns was born on 29 January instead of 25 January, so held their celebration four days late. Thankfully, a year later they discovered the parish records, which revealed Burns's date of birth as 25 January 1759, and Burns Night moved again, this time for good.

The central ingredients of the Burns Night supper were there, fully formed, at the earliest gatherings. As the *Burns Chronicle and Club Directory* reported of that inaugural 1801 commemoration, with wonderfully coy use of the word 'interesting': 'These nine sat down to a comfortable dinner, of which sheep's head and haggis formed an interesting part.' The address to the haggis, in which Burns's poem of that name is read aloud before the haggis is ceremonially carved, also featured, as did numerous readings from Burns's other work. But as the Burns scholar Murray Pittock has observed, the men in attendance at that first Burns supper were freemasons, which helps to explain why the ritualistic form of Burns Night has a whiff of the masons about it.

Burns's influence on subsequent writers, including songwriters, has been considerable. His poem 'A Red, Red Rose' was the young Bob Dylan's biggest source of creative inspiration. His work inspired the titles of several classic twentieth-century American novels: both John Steinbeck's *Of Mice and Men* and J. D. Salinger's *The Catcher in the Rye* owe their titles to Burns's poems. Steinbeck knew Burns's poem 'To a Mouse', which describes the poet's sadness and sense of remorse over having destroyed the mouse's habitat when ploughing a field.

The ship the *Cutty Sark*, by the way, also gets its name from a Burns poem: Cutty Sark is the nickname of the witch Nannie Dee in Burns's poem 'Tam o' Shanter' (a title which itself gave its name to a type of cap worn in Scotland). Burns's influence on the language is everywhere. He also provides the dictionary with the earliest known uses of the words 'auntie', 'blether', 'flunkey', 'inescapable', 'magnum', 'nouveau-riche', 'tricky', and 'uncaring'.

Burns is honoured with numerous statues around the world: after Queen Victoria and Christopher Columbus, he has more statues dedicated to him than any other non-religious person.

Great Scott at Abbotsford House

Robert Burns may have more statues dedicated to him than any other writer, but he doesn't have the largest monument in his own home country. Instead, that honour goes to another giant of Scottish literature, Sir Walter Scott (1771–1832), a memorial to whom stands in Princes Street Gardens in Edinburgh, a stone's throw from Waverley railway station (which is named after one of Scott's novels) and not too far from Tynecastle, the home ground of the football team Heart of Midlothian (named after another of Scott's novels). At nearly 62 metres in height, the Scott Monument is the largest monument to a writer in the whole world.

Much of Scott's work was hugely popular during his lifetime, yet he seems to have had a feeling that his writing would not necessarily last. At Abbotsford, as Stuart Kelly records in his fascinating *Scott-Land: The Man Who Invented a Nation*, the author of *Waverley* planted acres of trees. 'I promise you, my oaks will outlast my laurels,' he wrote to a friend, 'and I pique myself more upon my compositions for manure than on any other compositions whatsoever to which I was ever accessory.' Certainly, Scott seemed to view literature as a profession rather than an art, and considered military achievements far worthier of laurels than mere novels.

Scott was a sort of one-man marketing campaign for his country. With his design for his vast home, Abbotsford, near the River Tweed, he essentially invented modern-day Scottish tourism. The house was crammed full with relics from the author's own novels, as Kelly observes: a lock of Bonnie Prince Charlie's hair (a nod to *Waverley*), a fragment of a dress that had once belonged to Mary, Queen of Scots (who features in *The Abbot*), and even the doorway to the Old Tolbooth prison in Edinburgh, the jail that had housed the accused child-murderer Effie Deans in Scott's *The Heart of Midlothian*. The house was like a museum to a writer who hadn't got round to dying yet.

Many high-profile visitors to Scott's mansion detested it. John Ruskin asserted that Scott had 'some confused love of Gothic architecture, because it was dark, picturesque, old, and like nature; but he could not tell the worst from the best, and built for himself perhaps the most incongruous and ugly pile that gentlemanly modernism ever designed'. The actor William Macready called it 'a monument of his vanity and indiscretion'. Scott was able to enjoy living in the finished Abbotsford for just a year, before the debts he'd accrued in building the place forced him to move out.

Despite the mixed reviews Abbotsford received, it helped to revive the architectural style known as Scottish Baronial. And Scott was in many ways the father of the Scottish tourist industry. In 1822, he masterminded King George IV's visit to Scotland, and in the process helped to create a national myth. The former Prince Regent arrived clad in a kilt and a ridiculous amount of tartan, sparking a national fad.

The Goatherd-Poet of Jarrow

Let's leave Abbotsford in Scotland behind and go in search of some abbots in England. This may be trickier than it sounds. In the year 664, according to the Venerable Bede, a 'sudden pestilence' swept through Britain and Ireland, 'raging far and wide with fierce destruction'. It carried off numerous monks and abbots at monasteries in northern England, and at Bede's own monastery at Jarrow, he reports that all of the choir monks perished, with only the abbot and a small boy left alive. This plague was as devastating to the British population as the later, more famous Black Death of the fourteenth century. And, just as English poetry entered a golden age in the wake of the Black Death – Chaucer, John Gower, William Langland, and the *Gawain* poet were all writing in the decades following the most virulent epidemic – the birth of English poetry appears to have coincided with this earlier plague outbreak of the 660s.

Bede (672–735), also known as Saint Bede and the Venerable Bede, is best known for his *Historia ecclesiastica gentis Anglorum*, or *History of the English Church and People*, which he completed in 731. The book charts the establishment of Christianity in the British Isles, particularly in England, but he was a prolific author and chronicler who wrote around sixty other books in addition to his *History*. Even more remarkably, given the Viking raids on the British Isles which followed shortly after Bede's death, most of his books have survived.

Bede is often called the father of English history, and for good reason. We use the term 'Anno Domini' or 'AD' when talking about chronology because of him – not because he devised it, but because his adoption of this system of dating, which was proposed by Dionysius Exiguus, ensured that it would be taken up by later historians, and become the standard.

It is also thanks to Bede that we have *Cædmon's Hymn*, the oldest surviving Anglo-Saxon poem and, perhaps, the very first poem composed in the English language in England. It's just nine lines and forty-two words long, but it represents the beginning of English literature written in the vernacular:

> Nu scylun hergan hefaenricaes uard
> metudæs maecti end his modgidanc
> uerc uuldurfadur swe he uundra gihwaes
> eci dryctin or astelidæ
> he aerist scop aelda barnum
> heben til hrofe haleg scepen.
> tha middungeard moncynnæs uard
> eci dryctin æfter tiadæ
> firum foldu frea allmectig

This might not look much like English, although several words, such as *æfter* ('after') and *allmectig* ('almighty'), are recognisable. The poem can be translated as follows: 'Now we must honour the guardian of heaven, the might of the architect, and his purpose, the work of the father of glory as he, the eternal lord, established the beginning of wonders; he first created for the children of men heaven as a roof, the holy creator then the guardian of mankind, the eternal lord, afterwards appointed the middle earth, the lands for men, the Lord almighty.' Which also tells us that Cædmon, and not Tolkien, invented 'middle earth'.

Who was Cædmon, and how did he come to write the first English poem? He was a seventh-century goatherd who, according to Bede, wrote much else besides his famous *Hymn* – though none of his other compositions has survived. Indeed, we only have the *Hymn* because of Bede, who preserved a Latin translation of the poem in his *Historia ecclesiastica gentis Anglorum*. Even then, Bede's rendering of the hymn was in Latin, but thankfully some anonymous scribe added the Anglo-Saxon version of the poem in the margins of the manuscript of Bede's book. Thanks to Bede, and the anonymous writer who translated it, we have one of the earliest works of what we can call 'English poetry'. And it really was early. The seventh-century Cædmon is more remote from Chaucer than Chaucer, in the fourteenth century, is from us. It really was a long time ago.

It's a sobering thought that if Bede had never mentioned Cædmon or written down his poem, we would never have heard of him. As it is, we know a fair bit about him. Cædmon worked at the monastery of Streonæshalch, or Whitby Abbey, during the time of St Hilda (614–680). Bede tells us that Cædmon was ignorant of 'the art of song' until a dream he had one night brought him the gift. Thankfully, the 'gift' proved more valuable than William McGonagall's would over a millennium later. If you want to make your pilgrimage to the birthplace of English poetry, at St Mary's Churchyard in Whitby a memorial commemorates Cædmon's role as the originator of English religious verse: 'To the glory of God and in memory of

Cædmon the father of English Sacred Song. Fell asleep hard by, 680.'

But, as we will see if we linger in this churchyard a while longer, not everyone who 'falls asleep' into death fails to wake up again.

Whitby and the Birth of Dracula

In the same churchyard in which you can find Cædmon's memorial, you can also follow in the footsteps of one of the most iconic fictional characters ever created: Dracula, the most filmed fictional character in the history of cinema and the chief poster-boy of the Undead.

In a strange way, we have Sir Henry Irving, the first British actor to be knighted, to thank for the Whitby connection to *Dracula* – and, perhaps, for the fact that *Dracula* exists at all. It was Irving who suggested that Bram Stoker, the Irish author of the novel, take a holiday to the seaside town, and it was Stoker's visit to Whitby that gave him many of the central ingredients of the novel. In 1890, Stoker, who was Irving's manager, had just finished an exhausting and not altogether successful tour of Scotland. The two men agreed to take a month off to recharge their batteries, and Irving suggested that Stoker head to Whitby. (Irving knew the town well because, somewhat surprisingly, he'd once run a circus there.)

Abraham 'Bram' Stoker duly rented rooms on the Royal Crescent and set about getting a bit of rest and relaxation in Whitby. It was while he was roaming the town that Stoker began to dream up the details of his novel. It was in Whitby library that Stoker encountered the name Dracula – meaning 'son of the dragon' – and thought it might be a good name for a character in a horror novel. In Stoker's novel, Count Dracula arrives in Britain at Whitby, in the shape of a black dog, when a Russian schooner, the *Demeter*, runs aground. Here, Stoker was drawing on a real event of 1885 involving the *Dmitry*, a ship that ran aground on Tate Hill Sands, a stone's throw from Whitby Abbey.

Mina Murray, in the novel, describes the abbey – founded by Hilda in the seventh century, around the time that Cædmon was herding goats and receiving divine inspiration for his *Hymn* – as 'a most noble ruin, of immense size, and full of beautiful and romantic bits; there is a legend that a white lady is seen in one of the windows'. But the most chilling thing occurs in the nearby churchyard:

> For a moment or two I could see nothing, as the shadow of a cloud obscured St Mary's Church. Then as the cloud passed I could see the ruins of the Abbey coming into view; and as the edge of a narrow band of light as sharp as a sword-cut moved along, the church and the churchyard became gradually visible . . . it seemed to me as though something dark stood behind the seat where the white figure shone, and bent over it. What it was, whether man or beast, I could not tell.

Such a passage was a result of Stoker's time in Whitby, but it was also from Whitby that he got the name of his famous vampire. If he hadn't holidayed there, we might now be reading a novel named *Count Wampyr* – the original, terrible name Stoker was considering for his character. Or, more likely, we wouldn't be reading a novel named that either, since even if it had been published it would probably have sunk without trace.

Shandy Hall

While we're on the topic of the dead and Undead, spare a thought for another Irish author, Laurence Sterne. Even after he died people couldn't leave him alone.

He'd not had a particularly good start in life. Born in Ireland in 1713, Sterne was a weak child who suffered from tuberculosis. He lost his father, Roger Sterne, at a young age when he was killed in a duel fought over a goose. It was only thanks to his rich relations, notably his kindly uncle, that Sterne managed to go to Cambridge and, following his graduation, to secure a living in the Church. (On the side, however, Sterne enjoyed getting up to all sorts of wicked and dissolute activities with a group of hellraisers named the Demoniacs.) He became an accomplished vicar whose sermons proved hugely popular. And the church would provide him with fodder for his first novel, a comic satire on a church feud, which was published in 1759 but proved so controversial that it was almost immediately suppressed. Undaunted, Sterne began writing his masterpiece, *Tristram Shandy*, but it was rejected for publication. Sterne decided to self-publish the book. Meanwhile, his wife was seriously ill, having suffered a nervous breakdown, adding to his domestic pressures and responsibilities. Yet he got *Tristram Shandy* into print, and it quickly became the book of the moment.

Not everyone liked it: Samuel Johnson later called it out as a passing fad, declaring, 'Nothing odd will do long.

Tristram Shandy did not last.' And Sterne, living in obscurity in North Yorkshire, had no idea how well the book was selling in London. But when he travelled down to the capital and tried to locate a copy, he found it impossible to track one down – because all the bookshops had sold out.

Following the success of *Tristram Shandy*, Sterne made his home at Shandy Hall, named after the most popular of his novels, which he finished writing at the small North Yorkshire village of Coxwold. The word 'shandy', by the way, is a Yorkshire dialect word meaning 'wild' or 'half-crazy', though how that came to be attached to the name of the drink nobody is quite sure. It's derived from 'shandy-gaff', but nobody knows where that comes from either. At any rate, the word wasn't used until the nineteenth century; originally, it denoted a mixture of beer and ginger beer, rather than lemonade.

Sterne lived at Shandy Hall for eight years before his poor health finally did for him in 1768. He was buried in London, but grave-robbers reportedly dug up his body and sold it to a surgeon for an anatomy lecture. The story goes that Sterne's corpse was only rescued when someone in the audience recognised the hapless author lying on the dissecting table.

Sterne was promptly reburied, but a couple of centuries later he was dug up again, this time by the Laurence Sterne Trust, who wanted to save the body from further disturbance after his burial ground was sold for redevelopment. He was duly interred in his beloved Coxwold. Or at least, he may have been. Those who exhumed him claimed it was difficult to tell which bones were Sterne's and which belonged to somebody else, so in the end the skull that was judged the likeliest match for Sterne's was placed in the new grave at Coxwold. (This story of burial grounds and skulls is suitably Shandean, and a fitting sequel to the life of the man who gave us a character named Parson Yorick.)

With *Tristram Shandy*, did Sterne invent modernism 150 years before modernism – before the stream-of-consciousness style of James Joyce, Virginia Woolf, and Katherine Mansfield? In one sense, he certainly prefigures modernism in the way his narrator moves from one subject to another: in one notable passage, his meditation on sleep leads him to muse on buttonholes, and then on Sancho Panza, much as our minds like to dart from one thing to the next. And yet with his larger-than-life characters blessed with such names as Dr Slop, Parson Yorick, and Widow Wadman, his work bears the firm stamp of the eighteenth century. But it's revealing that the novel found admirers among some of the leading philosophers of the nineteenth century, including Schopenhauer and Marx. Indeed, a teenage Karl Marx even wrote a short (and still unpublished) novel, *Scorpion and Felix*, which bears the influence of Sterne's novel.

Shandy Hall is a monument to the popularity of the novel which gave the house its name, a novel that stands alone among eighteenth-century works because of its novelty and proto-modernist inventiveness.

The Prophetess of Knaresborough

Laurence Sterne may be buried at Shandy Hall, but we can't be sure – but then sometimes it doesn't matter that we cannot say for sure whether someone was actually buried, or born, in a certain place. Legend becomes fact. A good example of this can be seen at what was, effectively, the very first commercial tourist attraction in England.

Coming down to the small town of Knaresborough near Harrogate, we can find the unlikely tourist attraction known as Mother Shipton's Cave – which is not far from a petrifying well (that is, one that gives objects a stony appearance) which landowners began charging visitors to see in 1630. But it is the nearby cave named after England's most famous prophetess that concerns us here.

Legend says that Mother Shipton was born in the cave, but legend has a habit of making things up as it goes. Indeed, Mother Shipton may never have been born anywhere, because she may never have existed at all. Like another great figure of folklore, Robin Hood (who also has an association with Yorkshire), the case for a real-life Mother Shipton is far from watertight. But like that petrifying well, time has a habit of giving insubstantial details the illusion of being set in stone.

The *Oxford Dictionary of National Biography* entry on Yorkshire's foremost soothsayer describes her as a 'mostly legendary figure', the product – like Robin Hood or King Arthur – of a series of revisions and additions made by writers, historians, and good old-fashioned gossip and hearsay. The first written reference to her is not until some eighty years after her supposed death, when in 1641 some of her predictions were published in *The Prophesie of Mother Shipton in the Raigne of King Henry the Eighth*. She is supposed to have been born Ursula Southeil in Knaresborough in around 1488, and to have been extraordinarily ugly – so hideous, in fact, that a species of moth bearing a pattern on its wings that resembles her hook-nosed profile has been named in her honour, if 'honour' is quite the right word here. But many of the details about her life came from one book by a man named Richard Head in 1667, and how much of it he made up (some scholars, such as Arnold Kellett, say virtually all of it) remains a real question among historians and biographers.

A subsequent edition of Mother Shipton's prophecies published in 1684 introduced the story of her having been born in the Yorkshire cave that now bears her name. Samuel Pepys recorded in his diary in October 1666 that she had supposedly predicted the Great Fire of London, and the 1641 edition of her prophecies had stated that she had foreseen Cardinal Wolsey's downfall and death before he reached the city of York in 1530. But nobody seems to be quite sure of exactly what she *did* predict. In one famous case, she is purported to have prognosticated that 'the world to an end will come / in eighteen hundred and eighty-one', but it was later revealed that the actual author of these words was a Victorian book dealer named Charles Hindley. At any rate, when 1881 came and went, and the world was still very much in existence on New Year's Day 1882, later editions of 'her' work retained the couplet but quietly altered the year of apocalypse to 1991 (for some reason, it had to be a palindromic year). She's also been credited with predicting both the steam engine and the electric telegraph, despite the fact that these technological forecasts didn't appear in editions of her work until 1862, by which time both inventions had already well and truly arrived on the scene.

In short, then, Mother Shipton's reputation as Britain's greatest prophetess was largely the invention of a Victorian man. But her distinctive appearance – even if it was also a posthumous invention – inspired later incarnations of her as both a pipe-smoking puppet and as an early model for the pantomime dame. Her putative birthplace even turned into an unlikely site of pilgrimage. Mother Shipton became something the good woman herself could not even have foreseen: she became a brand.

York's Poetry Window

As we reach the city of York (something, as Mother Shipton foresaw, that Wolsey never managed), I think it's time for a quick breather on this tour of literary Britain, and a quick quiz. What was the most popular English poem of the Middle Ages? Chaucer's *Canterbury Tales*, perhaps? Or his *Troilus and Criseyde*? Or William Langland's *Piers Plowman*? Or the anonymous Arthurian poem *Sir Gawain and the Green Knight*?

The answer is none of these, but rather a poem from around 1350 called *The Pricke of Conscience*. The poem exists in more medieval manuscripts than any other poem: a total of 83 copies of Chaucer's *Canterbury Tales*, which was hugely popular almost immediately, survive from the Middle Ages and early Renaissance, but there are 115 manuscripts of *The Pricke of Conscience*. The *Pricke* is the forgotten 'bestseller' of medieval England. Nobody knows for sure who wrote it, though for many years it was attributed to Richard Rolle, a hermit and mystic who lived near the nunnery at Hampole, a small village north of Doncaster. Nowadays most medievalists credit the *Pricke* simply to Anonymous. The poem is written in the Northumbrian dialect.

In 9,000 lines of verse – that's over half the length of Chaucer's colossal *Canterbury Tales* – the author describes the nature of sin and the afterlife in ways that ordinary churchgoers could understand. Even those who were illiterate and uneducated could comprehend the poem's language and message, if it were read aloud to them by a priest. These days, Middle English presents a bit more of a challenge, though as the opening lines of the poem demonstrate, we can still make out the general gist, even without helpful glosses:

> The myȝt of þe fadir almyȝtty
> The wisdom of þe sone al wytty
> The grace and þe goodnesse of þe holi gost
> O god and oo lord of miȝt most

Which may not be so easy to read now, but in the mid fourteenth century was daringly vernacular when most religious poetry in England was still composed and recited in Latin.

What exactly was the message of *The Pricke of Conscience*? From one perspective it's Christian propaganda, displaying considerable learning – 'encyclopedic' is the word used by more than one scholar who's written about it – with its author entreating the reader to lead the good life and steer clear of sins of all kinds. If you should sin, then you jolly well need to repent. According to Byron Lee Grigsby in *Pestilence in Medieval and Early Modern English Literature*, the *Pricke* is one of only two medieval English poems to connect leprosy with lechery – usually, lepers were thought to have committed a spiritual sin rather than a carnal one (or, if they were lucky, more than one). But the poem considers, like Chaucer's later Parson's Tale, all seven deadly sins in turn. If you have sinned, you have to undergo due penance, both physically and mentally – hence the poem's title, combining as it does the visceral sting of a needle's prick with the more abstract notion of human conscience.

Although it appears to have been widely read in its day, the poem remains hard to get hold of in anything approaching an affordable scholarly edition. When James H. Morey brought out a new edition in 2012, he observed that the last one had been published the same year as the Battle of Gettysburg, nearly 150 years earlier. The *Pricke* is not a poem people – even medievalists – are rushing to read or to set on English literature courses.

Yet there is clear evidence that *The Pricke of Conscience* must have appealed to parishioners as well as the clergy, to laymen as well as the learned. And this brings us to York, one of the many places in England where the *Pricke* would have been popular. Indeed, in All Saints' Church, on North Street, it was so popular that you can see fifteen scenes from the poem – representing man's last fifteen days on earth – depicted in a stained-glass window dating from around 1410, along with accompanying quotations. It is poetry set to coloured glass, and it is beautiful – a little-known gem of medieval literature and art combined in one.

A Potter at Hill Top

In Near Sawrey in the Lake District, around a mile and a half to the west of Lake Windermere, you can visit Hill Top Farm, the home of Beatrix Potter from 1905 until her death nearly forty years later.

I say 'home', but in fact, although Hill Top has become the Beatrix Potter Museum, she was largely absent from the farm, living at the nearby Castle Cottage with her husband, William Heelis, following their marriage in 1913. Castle Cottage would be her *real* home, and the place where she died in 1943. But Potter kept Hill Top Farm, using the property as a place to work on her books, store her possessions, and breed sheep. (Among her more unlikely achievements, she could include 'president elect of the Herdwick Sheepbreeders' Association'.)

Indeed, Potter used her considerable wealth, generated by the colossal success of her children's books and by sales of her illustrations, to buy up local land on the condition that the National Trust bought half of it from her as soon as they'd raised the funds. (She did this with the Monk Coniston estate in 1930.) Her association with the National Trust was long-standing and she was friends with Canon Rawnsley, who was instrumental in the formation of the Trust in 1895. But the influence went both ways: it was also Rawnsley who encouraged her to complete her first book-length work for children, *The Tale of Peter Rabbit*. (However, he also thought the story would be better if it was told in rhyming couplets, and duly set about rewriting the book in verse that was, in the words of Beatrix Potter scholar Judy Taylor, 'startlingly banal'. Thankfully, this poetical offence was rejected by the publishers.)

Many bestselling children's authors had a rocky road to success. J. K. Rowling was rejected by a dozen publishers before her first *Harry Potter* novel found a home. Dr Seuss' first book was rejected by at least twenty publishers, and perhaps as many as forty-three; accounts vary. According to the author himself, he was walking home to burn the manuscript of his unwanted book when he bumped into an old classmate, who ended up getting the book into print. If that encounter had never happened, the world may never have heard of Dr Seuss. Between them, Rowling and Seuss have sold close to a billion books.

In the end, *The Tale of Peter Rabbit* was rejected by so many publishers that Potter decided to self-publish 250 copies and sell them herself. They soon sold out, devoured by eager friends and relations. The book has now sold 45 million copies, making it one of the biggest-selling children's books of all time. Potter drew on the local landscape for inspiration. She had first visited the Lake District on a family holiday in 1882 when she was a teenager living in London, and for much of the rest of her life she would remain attached to the area.

Helen Beatrix Potter – she was known by her middle name to distinguish her from her mother, who was also called Helen – was a delicate child and frequently ill. Her parents were well-off and there was no need for Beatrix to work, so she pursued her interest in the natural world (among other things, she wrote scientific papers on fungi), watercolour painting, and writing children's stories, many of which began life in letters she wrote to the sickly son of one of her governesses. Between 1881 and 1897, Potter kept a journal in code, which was discovered in 1952 and deciphered six years later, some fifteen years after her death.

After her marriage, Potter wrote hardly any further children's stories. The decade prior to this had seen the publication of her tales of Benjamin Bunny, Jeremy Fisher, Tom Kitten, Jemima Puddle-Duck, Samuel Whiskers, and numerous others, but after she became Mrs Heelis she shunned the limelight, turned down interviews, and even encouraged rumours that she'd died. When she did actually die in 1943, she was cremated in Blackpool and her ashes were scattered over her land – land that she had taken so much care to preserve and protect.

A Romantic from Cockermouth

Staying in the Lake District, we travel to Cockermouth, the Cumbrian town where William Wordsworth was born in 1770. He went to school here, at the Cockermouth Free School – the same school as Fletcher Christian, the man who would lead the mutiny on the *Bounty* in 1789. Christian was six years senior to Wordsworth.

Wordsworth was a keen walker among the Lakes. The critic and famous opium addict Thomas De Quincey once estimated that Wordsworth walked up to 180,000 miles in his whole life. Wordsworth may have lived to be eighty, but even if we're generous and claim all eighty years of his life as years of active walking, that's still well over 2,000 miles a year, or around 6 or 7 miles every day. But then De Quincey may have been under the influence of his beloved opium when he made his calculations.

The poem that is probably Wordsworth's most famous was inspired by the landscape of the Lake District. It's often referred to (erroneously, if we're being pedantic) as 'The Daffodils' or 'Daffodils', but in fact it had no title and is technically known only by its first line, 'I wandered lonely as a cloud'. On 15 April 1802, Wordsworth and his sister Dorothy were walking (there's a surprise) around Glencoyne Bay in Ullswater when they encountered, in the words of Dorothy's journal, a 'long belt' of daffodils:

we saw a few daffodils close to the water side, we fancied that the lake had floated the seed ashore & that the little colony had so sprung up – But as we went along there were more & yet more & at last under the boughs of the trees, we saw that there was a long belt of them along the shore, about the breadth of a country turnpike road. I never saw daffodils so beautiful they grew among the mossy stones about & about them, some rested their heads upon these stones as on a pillow for weariness & the rest tossed and reeled and danced & seemed as if they verily laughed with the wind that blew upon them over the Lake, they looked so gay ever dancing ever changing.

The dancing daffodils of William's poem, then, sprang from Dorothy's prose description. Perhaps Dorothy should be allowed a joint author credit? But even if we grant her role in the formation of the poem (and she clearly helped to inspire her brother's work) there is another woman who has an even stronger claim to 'co-author of the daffodils poem'.

Who is this other woman? Well, here's a question. Who wrote the following lines?

> They flash upon that inward eye
> Which is the bliss of solitude.

They come from Wordsworth's poem, but they weren't written by him: his wife, Mary Hutchinson, contributed them, as Wordsworth himself confirmed, adding that he thought these the best two lines in the whole poem. (By the way, there's no evidence to support the oft-repeated claim that Wordsworth originally had 'I wandered lonely as a cow' as his somewhat less promising opening line until Dorothy advised him to alter it to 'I wandered lonely as a cloud'. It's a nice story, but it's a myth, which appears to have originated in Conrad Aiken's 1952 novel *Ushant*.)

'I wandered lonely as a cloud' first appeared in print in 1807 in Wordsworth's *Poems in Two Volumes*, which received largely negative reviews. A young Byron, who elsewhere branded Wordsworth as 'Turdsworth', described it as 'puerile'. It's fair to say that the poem, and the volume in which it appeared, weren't an instant classic. Wordsworth died on 23 April 1850 – just over a fortnight after his eightieth birthday, and on the anniversary of Shakespeare's death some 234 years before. For the last seven years of his life he was Poet Laureate of the United Kingdom, though he wrote no official verses during this time.

Bradford's Great Literary Son

A statue of J. B. Priestley (1894–1984) stands outside the National Media Museum in his home town of Bradford. The city has honoured its most famous literary son in a number of ways: he was given the Freedom of the City in 1973, and the library at the University of Bradford is named after him. Throughout his life, Priestley was a proud Yorkshireman. (He was also an unlikely ladies' man, despite having what one acquaintance described as a 'potato face'.)

Bradford also gave John Boynton Priestley his first opportunity to see his name in print: the young author's first published work appeared in a local newspaper, the *Bradford Pioneer*, a publication funded by the Independent Labour Party which had been formed there in 1893. Priestley, who considered his home town the most progressive place in Britain, was a committed socialist, which led George Orwell to add Priestley's name to his 'list' of suspected Soviet sympathisers (though Orwell's notes suggest that he added Priestley only tentatively). Priestley's socialism runs throughout his work, which included novels as well as plays. Even his most enduring work, *An Inspector Calls*, is shot through with criticism of the way working-class people are treated in twentieth-century Britain.

Priestley once remarked that the class consciousness found elsewhere in Britain wasn't found – at least, not to such a pronounced degree – in Bradford, because the upper classes were non-existent in the city so the social pyramid lacked its 'apex'. Even wealthy wool merchants who earned or bought impressive titles and country estates would be addressed familiarly as 'Sam' or 'Joe' by the local workers. This, for Priestley, is what made Bradford distinctive. It also arguably helps to explain why Priestley, as a son of Bradford, was able to write so well for the middle classes about working-class struggles.

Priestley didn't reach the middle classes through his plays alone: his wartime broadcasts were also hugely important. In fact, his Sunday night *Postscripts* broadcasts for BBC radio during the Second World War had an audience of some 16 million listeners, making him arguably the second most important wartime broadcaster in Britain after Winston Churchill. Priestley also wrote the first play ever to be televised, the romantic comedy *When We Are Married*, which was shown on television in 1938.

But he was also an experimenter, and as well as exploring class, his plays are full of his interest in the way time works. Priestley's 'Time Plays' – which are usually understood to comprise *Dangerous Corner*, *Time and the Conways*, *I Have Been Here Before*, and *Johnson Over Jordan*, but also sometimes include *When We Are Married* – are notable for their experimental treatment of the nature of time. *Johnson Over Jordan* is like a Yorkshire version of *It's a Wonderful Life*: after his death, the ordinary businessman Robert Johnson has to review his life before he can earn peace and be released from the spiritual limbo in which he is trapped. Each of the 'Time Plays' experiments with a different theory about time, many of them influenced by the work of the philosopher J. W. Dunne (who would also inspire C. S. Lewis and J. R. R. Tolkien to write short works of fiction influenced by his ideas). *Dangerous Corner*, which was adapted for film in 1934, centres on a chance remark made by a guest about a cigarette box at a dinner party, which sets in motion a chain of revelations. At the end of the play, however, time spools back to the start of the evening, the guest doesn't make his ill-advised remark, and none of the revelations comes to light. *Sliding Doors* for the 1930s, perhaps. *Dangerous Corner* was revived for the London stage in 2014.

Priestley was also a founder member of the Campaign for Nuclear Disarmament (CND). In November 1957 he wrote an article for the *New Statesman* titled 'Britain and the Nuclear Bombs', and the letter proved popular with so many readers that the CND was set up shortly after this, with Priestley on the board alongside other notable figures including the philosopher Bertrand Russell and the journalist and Labour politician Michael Foot.

Look Back at Morecambe

Of all the unusual places to sit and write a classic, John Osborne's choice of location must be one of the most surprising. Vladimir Nabokov and Gertrude Stein both liked to write while sitting in a parked car, though presumably not together. Truman Capote would often write while lying on his back, with a glass of sherry in one hand and a pencil in the other. But John Osborne wrote much of his seminal play *Look Back in Anger* over the course of seventeen days while sitting in a deckchair on Morecambe pier.

At this stage of his life, Osborne was living in a tiny flat in Derby with his wife, the actress Pamela Lane. The marriage was not especially happy – the couple would separate shortly afterwards – and the home life of Jimmy and Alison Porter in *Look Back in Anger* sprang from Osborne's own wedded misery. (Pamela was also having an affair with a dentist, getting more than her teeth seen to, one suspects. Ironically, Osborne, who was an actor as well as a playwright, had recently played a dentist in a production of a George Bernard Shaw play.)

When he wrote *Look Back in Anger*, Osborne was unknown as a playwright and wasn't much better known as an actor. The repertory life meant frequent travelling all over the country, and Osborne would spend any spare time he had in public libraries during the winter months, and on seaside piers during the summer. As John Heilpern reveals in his illuminating biography, these piers became 'his open-air office'. It was while he was playing a small role in a play for the Morecambe Rep in 1955 that Osborne wrote most of the second act of the play that would not only transform his own career, but revitalise the stagnant British theatre of the time. And he did it at the end of a pier.

It's clear that *Look Back in Anger* sent shockwaves through British theatre, blowing apart old attitudes, because the muscular language of Jimmy Porter's speeches in the play – which centres on Porter's failing marriage to Alison – attacked 1950s austerity Britain as, if you like, no country for young men. But in fact when it made its debut in London in May 1956, it met with what were, on the whole, quietly negative reviews. That soon started to change, however. First, the theatre critic and *enfant terrible* Kenneth Tynan wrote a glowing review of the play for the *Observer*, declaring that Osborne was the spokesman for a generation. Then the BBC showed an eighteen-minute excerpt from the play, and people flocked to see it. The play went on to become the defining dramatic work of the decade, capturing the national mood. According to the theatre critic Michael Billington, Osborne was also responsible for a shift in publishing, since Faber & Faber's decision to print the play-text of *Look Back in Anger* reintroduced the idea that publishing plays could be a serious and lucrative publishing venture. Osborne himself became a household name. Those seventeen days on Morecambe pier were well spent.

Haworth: Home of the Brontës

Many famous writers didn't get on well at school. In 1945 John Osborne had himself been expelled from Belmont College, a Devon boarding school, for punching the head-master, who had caught the young Osborne listening to a Frank Sinatra radio broadcast. Other writers received less than promising school reports. One of Roald Dahl's reports read, 'I have never met anybody who so persistently writes words meaning the exact opposite of what is intended.' Charlotte Brontë's entry report for the local school said she 'writes indifferently' and 'knows nothing of grammar, geography, history, or accomplishments'. It's true that the road to literary success was a slow one for her. As Charlotte wrote in a letter of March 1845: 'I shall soon be 30 – and I have done nothing yet . . . I feel as if we were all buried here.' A year later, when the Brontë sisters published a volume of poetry, *Poems by Currer, Ellis and Acton Bell*, it sold a grand total of just two copies.

Charlotte's talk of being 'buried here' was also grimly apt given the singularly insalubrious nature of her surroundings. Life in Haworth was tough. A sanitary report on the village written in 1850 revealed that the average life expectancy for the inhabitants was just twenty-five. Over forty per cent of children died before the age of six. This has been blamed on poor sanitation, which provided a breeding ground for cholera, typhus, dysentery, and other diseases which tried their best to ensure you didn't live to celebrate your thirtieth birthday (which Charlotte and Emily, unlike their sister Anne, managed to do). The Brontë children, clearly not in possession of a robust constitution, were more or less doomed in such an environment.

Despite the deleterious effect Haworth was to have on their health, the Brontë children treasured the wildness of the Yorkshire countryside, and none more so than Emily. 'Emily loved the moors,' Charlotte later wrote, 'they were what she lived in and by as much as the wild birds, their tenants, or the heather, their produce . . . She found in the bleak solitude many and dear delights; and not the least and best loved was – liberty.' It was this wild landscape that inspired Emily's one novel, *Wuthering Heights* (1847) – the unusual adjective in the book's title being a Yorkshire dialect word meaning 'rushing or whizzing'. (Pleasingly, the novel also brought the local word 'gormless' to the attention of the wider world.) Emily is thought to have based Wuthering Heights on Top Withens, a real farmhouse in Yorkshire.

Initially, reviewers didn't know what to make of *Wuthering Heights*. 'We rise from the perusal of *Wuthering Heights* as if we had come fresh from a pest-house', one reviewer wrote, before going on to recommend burning the book as the best course of action. 'How a human being could have attempted such a book as the present without committing suicide before he had finished a dozen chapters, is a mystery', another remarked, with an almost visible shake of the head. The *North British Review* simply said that 'the only consolation which we have in reflecting upon it is that it will never be generally read'. Even Charlotte, defending but also criticising her sister's novel following Emily's death in 1848, felt the need to apologise for the 'rude and strange' nature of the book, which she attributed to her sister's rural northern upbringing. Emily died believing her only novel was a critical failure.

Charlotte, surviving Anne and Emily by several years, was the only one of the sisters to marry, doing so in 1854 when she wedded a young Ulsterman named Arthur Bell Nicholls who had become curate at Haworth. Charlotte's father didn't approve of the match, hounding Arthur out of his job and refusing to attend his sole surviving daughter's wedding at Haworth. However, when the newly-wed couple returned from their honeymoon in Ireland, Mr Brontë did reappoint his new son-in-law as his curate. Within nine months of the marriage Charlotte was dead. Mr Brontë had lived to bury all six of his children. He himself died in 1861, having never read *Wuthering Heights*.

Knutsford to Cranford

Knutsford (named after Canute) is the model for Cranford in the series of interlinked stories of that name written by Elizabeth Gaskell (1810–65), one of the Victorian era's greatest realist writers. Gaskell was also Charlotte Brontë's first biographer: published in 1857, two years after Charlotte's death, *The Life of Charlotte Brontë* is considered one of the greatest Victorian literary biographies. Her fellow novelist Margaret Oliphant described it as a new kind of biography – more than this, it is 'for every woman dropped out of sight'. Gaskell herself has never dropped out of sight, with her novels still being read, studied, and adapted around the world. Her interlinked set of tales set in Cranford was brought to the small screen by the BBC in 2007.

Cranford is largely based on Gaskell's childhood re-collections of the Cheshire town: although she was born (as Elizabeth Stevenson) in London, she was brought to Knutsford shortly after her first birthday, after her mother died, to be raised by her aunt. She would remain in the town for the next twenty years, until her marriage to William Gaskell in 1832, whereupon she moved to Manchester. If her mother had lived, she may never have moved up north and might never have become a novelist.

Indeed, another death in the family – this time, tragi-cally, of a child rather than a parent – was responsible for inspiring Gaskell to take up her pen in the first place. She began writing in order to console herself when she was grieving for her son, Willie, who died of scarlet fever in 1845. Gaskell set about writing her first novel, *Mary Barton*, her 'tale of Manchester life'. It was published in 1848 to huge acclaim.

When she wasn't writing realist fiction about the harsh realities of life in northern cities or penetrating and pithy stories about provincial life ('penetrating' and 'pithy' were Charlotte Brontë's words to describe *Cranford*), Gaskell was writing a range of other stories, including the little-known 1859 tale 'The Half-Brothers' featuring a collie dog named Lassie, which saves the day at the end of the story, thus prefiguring – if not actively inspiring – one of the twentieth century's most iconic canine film characters. (Pleasingly, the story even features the line 'Lassie came home'.) Gaskell also wrote a novella, *Lois the Witch* (1861), set against the backdrop of the 1692 Salem witch trials in America.

Gaskell died in 1865, aged fifty-five, from a heart attack. She was buried in the graveyard of Brook Street Unitarian Chapel in Knutsford, not far from the railway station where Captain Brown is killed in *Cranford* when he steps in front of the train to save a child (and not, as is often repeated, because he's too absorbed in reading *The Pickwick Papers*). In September 2010, for the bicentenary of her birth, Gaskell was commemorated with a memorial panel in Poets' Corner, Westminster Abbey.

Having Words in Manchester

There's an old quip: 'What's another word for a thesaurus?' In fact, there is another word for a thesaurus and what's more, there always has been: synonymicon. Next time someone rolls out that old line, you can respond by telling them that. It might not make you the most popular person at a party, but fans of word trivia (and that's all of us, right?) will love you for it. And, simultaneously, hate you. At any rate, it'll stop that person trotting out that old thesaurus gag again.

In fact, the word 'thesaurus' came to be applied to a book of synonyms because of one man, whose name is forever linked to this genre of book: Peter Mark Roget. In the world of dictionaries we talk of Webster's or Johnson's or Chambers', but 'thesaurus' belongs to Roget alone. Aptly, the terms 'Roget' and 'thesaurus' have become synonymous.

Thesauri (to give the word its correct plural) existed before Roget published his book, but they were known as synonymicons: in his 1813 book *English Synonyms Discriminated*, William Taylor uses this word to describe his dictionary of synonyms. Similarly, the word 'thesaurus' had been knocking around for a while – meaning a storehouse or receptacle for treasure and, from the sixteenth century, a dictionary or encyclopaedia – but it would not be until 1852 that the word would be applied specifically to a book of synonyms, when Peter Mark Roget published the work that has become known as *Roget's Thesaurus*.

Having said that, by the time it was published Roget had been at work on his thesaurus for almost half a century, since 1805 when he was a young medical professional working in Manchester. Although he wasn't resident in the city for long, it was while he was in Manchester that the idea for his thesaurus began to take root. In 1804, he became chief surgeon at the Manchester Infirmary. Two years later, he became the first secretary of the Portico Library on Mosley Street – whose chairman was later William Gaskell, husband of the novelist – and he was also a Vice President of the Manchester Literary and Philosophical Association.

Roget had been born in London in 1779, the son of a Swiss clergyman. He suffered from bouts of depression throughout his life, and it's not hard to see why. It seems to have been in his genes – his mother was prone to paranoia, and one of his grandmothers may have had schizophrenia – and a series of tragic events involving other family members can't have helped. His father died young, as did his wife. In 1818, when Roget was thirty-nine, his uncle committed suicide by cutting his throat in his nephew's presence. List-making – specifically, compiling lists of words with similar meanings to each other – appears to have been Roget's way of coping with the blacker periods in his life, of bringing order to a chaotic and unpredictable world. It was only once he retired that he turned to the task of publishing the book that had been his life's work.

The original edition of *Roget's* is a valuable source of colourful words and phrases which have long fallen out of use. Under 'sensualist', for example, as well as 'Sybarite' and 'voluptuary' we find 'Sardanapalus' (from the legend surrounding an Assyrian king who supposedly passed his entire life in luxury and self-indulgence) and, even more intriguingly, 'carpet knight'. Under 'gluttony' (on the same page; Roget grouped his words together by concept, so it worked as a kind of dictionary in reverse) we find the useful idioms 'have the stomach of an ostrich' and 'play a good knife and fork'. Under 'flatterer', we find 'claw-back', 'ear-wig', 'pickthank', and, most majestically of all, 'Sir Pertinax MacSycophant'. You can open up the original *Roget's* at virtually any page and find such vivid terms waiting to be revived.

As Roget announced in the book's preface, his thesaurus was compiled for 'those who are unpractised in the art of composition, or unused to extempore speaking' and to offer 'a helping hand' to 'those who are thus painfully groping their way and struggling with the difficulties of composition'. The book was an instant hit, going through twenty-eight printings in the seventeen years between its initial publication and Roget's death in 1869. To date, it has sold over 40 million copies, with successive editions adding new words to its vocabulary ('masturbation' made a controversial arrival among its pages in 2002, while the list of phobias included has grown a great deal). J. M. Barrie was one of many writers who owed a debt to him: indeed, the *Peter Pan* creator had the Darling family live in a square in Bloomsbury because that's where Roget lived for a while when in London, and, as Barrie remarked, 'we whom he has helped to wend our way through life have always wanted to pay him a little compliment'. Sylvia Plath referred to herself as 'Roget's strumpet'.

The thesaurus wasn't Roget's only lasting achievement. He was a founder of the Manchester Medical School and what became the Royal Society of Medicine, and was active in the formation of the University of London. Mathematicians, too, have been in his debt: in 1815, he invented the slide rule, which until the arrival of the calculator over a century later would be the calculating machine of choice for maths students everywhere. Roget's theories of optical illusion have even been credited with influencing the development of early cinema. But it's for his thesaurus that he is best known. Sufferers from monologophobia – fear of repeating the same word in a speech or piece of writing, for want of an alternative – have been grateful, appreciative, thankful, obliged, beholden, and indebted ever since.

Herman Melville in Liverpool

Liverpool has been a part of the British literary landscape since it was mentioned in a play from around 1590, which some people have attributed to Shakespeare. It's unlikely the Bard had a hand in it, but it's quite pleasing to think that he was responsible for putting Liverpool on the literary map with the words, 'Since fortune hath thus spitefully crost our hope, let us leave this quest and harken after our King, who is at this daie landed at Lirpoole'.

This inaugural mention of 'Lirpoole' appears in *Fair Em, the Miller's Daughter of Manchester*, a play which bears the intriguing subtitle, *With the Love of William the Conqueror*. When the play was written, both Manchester and Liverpool were relatively small towns – the latter had a population of around 2,000, and Manchester about twice that number – but they would later, of course, become vast cities with considerable literary reputations. Manchester gave the world *The Communist Manifesto*, *Mary Barton*, and, as we've already seen, *Roget's Thesaurus*.

Liverpool, meanwhile, has a host of literary associations. It was the place where the Victorian poet Arthur Hugh Clough was born and where his friend Matthew Arnold died. But some of the most notable literary links Liverpool can boast involve American writers. As Frank Morley remarks in *Literary Britain*, the New York writer Washington Irving 'owed the start of his successful career to Liverpool', if only because his failure to become a successful merchant in the city turned him to writing *The Sketch-Book*, which became a bestseller across the Atlantic in 1819. But Irving wasn't the only US writer to visit Liverpool. Harriet Beecher Stowe, Ralph Waldo Emerson, Nathaniel Hawthorne, and Herman Melville all docked in the city during the mid nineteenth century.

Melville stayed with Hawthorne in Liverpool, and described the city in 1849 as 'a port in which all climes and countries embrace'. The narrator of his novel *Redburn*, based on Melville's own experiences in the city, describes how an African American visitor or immigrant to Liverpool 'lifts his head like a man' because he doesn't face the prejudice he had to endure back in the States. Melville's narrator also recalls how he 'encountered our black steward, dressed very handsomely, and walking arm in arm with a good-looking English woman', something that would have been unthinkable in New York. There, 'such a couple would have been mobbed in three minutes; and the steward would have been lucky to escape with whole limbs'. Indeed, Liverpool would become the home of Britain's first substantial black community.

The Novelist of the Potteries

Stoke's literary fame is really down to one man, whose own name was immortalised in the name of an omelette.

Born in 1867 in Hanley, Staffordshire (part of the famous Potteries and now a district of Stoke-on-Trent), Enoch Arnold Bennett was named after his father, a solicitor. Enoch junior was sent to the school at Newcastle-under-Lyme (Oldcastle in his fiction); on Waterloo Road in Cobridge, Stoke, there is a blue plaque commemorating Bennett's childhood home. Arnold Bennett (like Beatrix Potter, he dropped his first name for publication) became a successful writer only after he had left his home town in the Potteries, but he would return to Stoke and its environs again and again in his fiction, branding them the Five Towns (actually a slight misnomer, since the area around Stoke was known in real life as the six towns) and writing about the ordinary folk who lived in the area. It is an odd fact in the life of Arnold Bennett that he could not perhaps have written so well about his homeland of North Staffordshire if he had remained there. Would James Joyce have been able to write *Ulysses* if he'd remained in Dublin?

In London, Bennett became a clerk to a solicitor and then, after winning a literary prize, a full-time journalist. He would continue to write journalism until his death in 1931, and towards the end of his life wrote a regular books column for the *Evening Standard*. His life would be a London one: the famous food dish which bears his name, omelette Arnold Bennett, comprising smoked haddock, cream, and Parmesan cheese, was invented by a chef at the Savoy Hotel where Bennett frequently dined. It is still on the menu there, and is served in many other restaurants.

Yet although his tales of Staffordshire life were once eagerly devoured by readers and made him comfortably rich, they are now little read. Arguably, his omelette is more famous than the books he wrote. Virginia Woolf was largely responsible for this. In the narrative of English literary history, as evinced by many university degree programmes, the Victorians give way to the Modernists – you go from Charles Dickens and Thomas Hardy to Virginia Woolf and James Joyce. This, of course, overlooks the writers who fell between these two big periods: the Edwardians. In her 1919 essay 'Modern Novels', Woolf poured scorn on the fiction of the Edwardian novelists – whom she branded 'materialist' for their privileging of external detail over interior psychological complexity – and mentions by name three writers whom she considers particular literary culprits: H. G. Wells, John Galsworthy, and Arnold Bennett. In the longer 1923 essay 'Mr Bennett and Mrs Brown', she expanded on her objections to Bennett's approach to writing novels (largely motivated by the negative review by Bennett of her own novel, *Jacob's Room*). Woolf won the literary war, and succeeded in more or less airbrushing Bennett's name out of literary history – at least, so far as the university syllabuses depict it.

In his 1992 study *The Intellectuals and the Masses*, the critic John Carey cast Arnold Bennett as his book's 'hero', portraying Bennett as the champion of the 'masses' against the intelligentsia such as Woolf's Bloomsbury Group.

There is arguably a regional angle to all this: although Bennett was a Londoner by adoption, he was a Midlands writer by birth, and there's a sense that the cosmopolitan writers who belonged to Woolf's in-crowd looked down on the Staffordshire novelist for his provincial origins.

Bennett is best remembered – in so far as he's remembered at all – for *Anna of the Five Towns*, *Clayhanger*, *Hilda Lessways*, and *The Old Wives' Tale*, but he also wrote a popular self-help book titled *How to Live on 24 Hours a Day*. Published in 1910, this curious tome sees Bennett suggesting ways in which one can get the most out of life. The book was especially aimed at those stuck in middle-of-the-road jobs – clerks and other white-collar professionals who constituted much of his substantial readership – whose daily routine was repetitive and whose work was uninspiring. The book prescribes reading, hobbies, and taking an interest in art, among other things, as ways to improve one's overall happiness. Chapters include 'The Daily Miracle', 'Dangers to Avoid', and, perhaps most intriguingly of all, 'Tennis and the Immortal Soul'. In 1918, Bennett refused a knighthood, offered partly for his services to the Ministry of Information during the First World War.

He died of typhoid in 1931 after drinking tap water in a Paris restaurant, despite being advised against doing so by the waiter. According to Robert Graves, in his final years Bennett had carried a crumpled five-pound note with him, to give to the first person he saw reading one of his books. When he died, the note was found, still neatly folded, in his wallet.

Samuel Johnson's Uttoxeter Penance

If you'd gone to Uttoxeter market on a rainy day in the early 1780s, you could have witnessed a singular sight: the foremost literary man of his age standing in the market-place for a whole hour, in the pouring rain. This is because Uttoxeter's most famous literary claim to fame is that it was the place where Samuel Johnson performed his 'penance', which largely consisted of standing about in the street getting very wet.

But then Johnson, an undoubtedly great man, was also a singularly odd one. According to his first – and still most celebrated – biographer, James Boswell, 'Doctor' Johnson (he only acquired the first of his honorary doctorates in 1765, ten years after his famous dictionary was published) would refuse to listen to anyone else at the dinner table until he had satisfied his appetite, 'which was so fierce, and indulged with such intenseness, that while in the act of eating, the veins of his forehead swelled, and generally a strong perspiration was visible'. These days, we might say he had an addictive personality: addicted quite possibly to drink, to eating, to reading (ever since he first read and fell under the spell of *Hamlet* as an eight-year-old, while living above his father's bookshop in Lichfield), and – above all – to work. He also collected bits of orange peel, possibly for some unknown medicinal remedy. (When Boswell pressed him for more details, the good doctor replied, 'Nay, Sir, you shall know their fate no further.')

Poor eyesight was also a cause of the Doctor's misfortunes. As a boy of three, he'd trodden on a duckling and later wrote an epitaph for it, his first literary composition: 'Here lies good master duck whom Samuel Johnson trod on.' Later in life he repeatedly came close to setting his wig on fire, from leaning too close to the candle while reading at night. And his other quirks were well noted. As a young man he was turned down for a teaching job because it was feared his 'way of distorting his face' would scare the pupils. However, this was perhaps more than eccentricity, since it's reckoned Johnson may have had Tourette's syndrome.

In short, Johnson had to overcome considerable difficulties on his road to becoming the greatest man of letters in the eighteenth century. But books – specifically, books in Uttoxeter – were also the cause of his penance, performed years later when Johnson was an old man. As a youth, he had refused to help run his father's bookstall in the town. As the universally renowned Doctor Johnson, he regretted having denied his father help, and so he went and stood, bareheaded in the pouring rain, on the spot in Uttoxeter marketplace where his father's bookstall had stood decades before. As Johnson himself described it: 'a postchaise to Uttoxeter, and going into the market at the time of high business, uncovered my head, and stood with it bare an hour before the stall which my father had formerly used, exposed to the sneers of the standers-by and the inclemency of the weather'.

The event is commemorated with a memorial, erected on the spot where Johnson stood. At the memorial each year, a ceremony is held to remember the day the good doctor allowed the weather and the locals to take him down a peg or two.

Robin of . . . Barnsdale?

Coming down into South Yorkshire, we find ourselves in Robin Hood country, namely the forest of . . . Barnsdale.

Or should that be Barnsdale, Rutland? Where are we? 'Robin Hood in Barnsdale stood', an old ballad from 1429 has it; the phrase was historically used in law courts when somebody was not speaking to the point, though quite why, nobody appears to know. Nor do we know which 'Barnsdale' this refers to. All we do know is that a number of early ballads and tales featuring the hooded thief (or social reformer, depending on your political bent) place Robin not in Sherwood Forest in Nottinghamshire, but in Barnsdale Forest in – well, either South Yorkshire or in Britain's smallest mainland county, Rutland, near Leicestershire. The greatest concentration of Robin Hood names in the whole of England is found not in Nottinghamshire at all, but in Wakefield and its environs – including the small village named Robin Hood, which lies exactly halfway between Wakefield and Leeds. In short, Robin is as much a Yorkshireman as a Nottinghamshire lad.

This is because it seems that from very early on, different regions rushed to claim Robin Hood as theirs, even before the modern tourist industry had evolved. The idea of Robin Hood as Robin of Locksley, the cheery Anglo-Saxon hero who had fought in the Crusades, is a surprisingly modern idea, dreamt up by Sir Walter Scott for his 1819 novel *Ivanhoe*. In Scott's novel we learn that Robin's name 'has been borne as far as Palestine', though as yet the Holy Land is about the only place that hasn't rushed to claim the Lincoln-greened one as their own. Presumably the name that had spread far and wide was 'Robin of Locksley' rather than the outlaw's alternative name in Scott's novel, 'Dickon Bend-the-Bow'.

It is hard to imagine a more influential nineteenth-century novel than *Ivanhoe*. The book's impact was instantaneous and far-reaching. John Henry Newman asserted that it 'had first turned men's minds in the direction of the middle ages', while Thomas Carlyle argued that Scott's novel had caused a revival of interest in history in general. Over in America, Mark Twain blamed Scott's novel for causing the American Civil War, because it had inspired a love of feudalism among the southern states. 'Sir Walter Scott had so large a hand in making Southern character, as it existed before the war,' Twain wrote in *Life on the Mississippi*, 'that he is in great measure responsible for the war.' In *Scott-Land: The Man Who Invented a Nation*, Stuart Kelly goes so far as to suggest that Scott's novel even influenced the rebuilding of the Palace of Westminster in the medieval Gothic, rather than Neoclassical, style.

But although the book is not read much now, its influence continued well into the twentieth century. Tony Blair and Ho Chi Minh both named *Ivanhoe* as their favourite novel. The town of Conisbrough, not far from Doncaster (home, of course, to Robin Hood Airport), is *Ivanhoe*-mad: it has a school named in honour of the novel, another school, Rowena Academy, named after one of the novel's two major love interests, and streets named Locksley Avenue and Scott Avenue. All of this is because of Scott's inclusion of a place named Coningsburgh in his novel.

The extraordinary success of *Ivanhoe* helped to cement the modern image of Robin Hood – a Saxon named Robin of Locksley, defending the absent Richard the Lionheart's kingdom from his evil brother John – in the popular consciousness. It also helped Scott to fund the building and development of his house, Abbotsford, which we encountered earlier on.

Interestingly, though, Scott was not the first Scottish writer to contribute substantially to the story of England's foremost mythical hero. An earlier writer, a Scottish historian named John Major (sometimes Maior or Mair), had been the first to place Robin in the 1190s, the reign of Richard the Lionheart, which would also provide the historical setting for Scott's novel (other writers and chroniclers tended to refer to a King Edward rather than Richard). In his *History of Greater Britain* (1521), Major wrote that 'about this time it was, as I conceive, that there flourished those most famous robbers Robert Hood, an Englishman, and Little John, who lay in wait in the woods, but spoiled of their goods those only that were wealthy'. Whereabouts 'Robert' and Little John plied their robbing trade, Major doesn't specify, but by the time Scott took up his pen some three centuries later, Robin's forest of choice had well and truly shifted from Barnsdale, wherever that was, to Sherwood.

Lawrence of Eastwood

Think of Nottinghamshire and the writer whose name immediately comes to mind is D. H. Lawrence, and for good reason.

Lawrence was Nottingham's son through and through. He was born in 1885 in Eastwood (the mining town became Bestwood in his highly autobiographical novel, *Sons and Lovers* (1913)), just three miles north of the city, and educated at both the high school and at University College (now the University of Nottingham).

However, two years before *Sons and Lovers*, Lawrence had published his first novel, *The White Peacock*, which was also set in his home town – which featured under the name Nethermere. *The White Peacock*, with its love triangle involving two men and one woman and the marital misery that ensues when the woman makes the 'wrong' choice, shows Lawrence's debt to Thomas Hardy. The novel was also loosely based on Lawrence's own experiences growing up in Eastwood, to the extent that the husband of a local woman, Alice Hall, threatened to take legal action against him for portraying his wife in the novel, somewhat unflatteringly, as Alice Gall.

The White Peacock also shows Lawrence's burgeoning interest in all things Freudian (he would later write a book, *Fantasia of the Unconscious*, about psychoanalysis). As John Sutherland points out in his *Lives of the Novelists*, the title, *The White Peacock*, doesn't just refer to the peacock which appears in the novel, but is a punning nod to the fact that a man's 'cock' is the only part of him that doesn't ever see sunlight, even when he pees – hence 'white pee-cock'. The early signs were there: after all, Lawrence would later write a story, 'Tickets, Please', featuring a cocky character named John Thomas (another nod to that part of a man's anatomy), and his working title of *Lady Chatterley's Lover* would be 'John Thomas and Lady Jane'.

But perhaps there's a more wholesome, local explanation for the title *The White Peacock*. Nearby Newstead Abbey, the Nottinghamshire home of Lord Byron a century before, is known for its peacocks: when Byron went travelling around Italy he took dogs, a pet bear, a monkey, and two white peacocks with him as part of his extensive menagerie. White peacocks are rare. In 2014, just over a century after Lawrence's novel appeared, a new white peacock hatched from an egg that had been bought on eBay, and was released into the grounds of the Nottinghamshire abbey. Byron, one suspects, would approve. Lawrence? Who can say.

A Mousetrap at Nottingham

On 6 October 1952 a new Agatha Christie play had its premiere at the Theatre Royal in Nottingham. Leading the cast were Sheila Sim and her husband Richard Attenborough. The play had begun life five years earlier as a short radio drama, *Three Blind Mice*, written to honour the eightieth birthday of Queen Mary, the widow of King George V. Christie turned this radio script into a short story, then into a stage play, but she had to change the title because a play named *Three Blind Mice* had been put on in the West End a few years earlier. Sticking with the murine theme, Christie's son-in-law suggested *The Mousetrap*, after the jokey nudge-nudge-wink-wink name Hamlet gives to the play-within-a-play in Shakespeare's Danish tragedy. And that was that.

Early signs hardly suggested the play was likely to prove the record-breaking smash hit it would go on to become. When *The Mousetrap* premiered, the *Manchester Guardian* called it a 'middling piece' with characters 'built entirely of clichés'. The *Daily Express* thought the characters 'too obvious by half'. Christie herself thought the play would be lucky to run for more than eight months. She bequeathed the rights to the play to her grandson, Matthew Prichard, for his ninth birthday. As birthday presents (or trust funds for nine-year-olds) go, it must certainly be one of the most financially lucrative.

After its premiere at Nottingham, *The Mousetrap* transferred to London, where it has remained – a handful of tours excepted – ever since, for over 25,000 performances with no signs of its popularity dwindling. In 1957, it overtook Noël Coward's record for the longest-running West End play (for *Blithe Spirit*), and the Savoy hotel held a party to celebrate, which Christie later branded 'Hell at the Savoy', not least because the porter didn't recognise her and initially turned her away from her own party.

Christie died in 1976, and two West End theatres – including St Martin's, where *The Mousetrap* is staged – dimmed their lights in her honour. Forty years on, on 19 January 2016, *The Mousetrap* returned to the Theatre Royal in Nottingham where it had premiered sixty-four years before. Earlier that day, Sheila Sim, star of the original cast in the same theatre, had passed away. The evening performance was dedicated to her. Richard Attenborough, the other leading cast member in the original production, had died in 2014. Those three blind mice are still running.

Larkin in Loughborough

The poet Philip Larkin (1922–85) is most famously associated with Hull, which he wrote about in 'Here'. A town that doesn't immediately spring to mind when contemplating Larkin is Loughborough, in Leicestershire, a town best known nowadays for its university. But Larkin spent much of his holiday time in Loughborough for over twenty years, and arguably his two most famous poems, 'The Whitsun Weddings' and 'This Be The Verse', have a Loughborough connection.

Although Larkin himself never lived in Loughborough, one street in the town, York Road, was home to two Larkins: the poet's older sister, Catherine, lived at number 53 for many years, while his mother moved into number 21 in 1951 after the death of Larkin's father, and continued to live there until 1972. Larkin would frequently visit, during university vacations and at weekends. Although he once described Loughborough as a dull town, he also reported in a letter to his long-term girlfriend Monica Jones that Loughborough seemed 'good, after Hull'. (Faint praise, that.) In the same letter, he mentions sampling a Stilton in the bar at the Kings Head, which is now the Ramada Jarvis Hotel on Derby Road. He also walked to Nanpantan, just south of the town, and had a pint of 'mouldy' beer, which sounds like a pretty typical Larkin experience.

But how did Loughborough influence the most popular English poet of the second half of the twentieth century?

It's difficult to ascertain, but it's possible that he wrote what is one of his most famous poems, 'This Be The Verse' (that's the one with the famous opening line about parents, featuring a certain four-letter word), while staying with his mother during the Easter 1971 vacation. And it's certainly true that 'Reference Back', written in 1955, details his visits to York Road in the early 1950s.

Many of Larkin's celebrated letters to his friend Kingsley Amis would be written from York Road in Loughborough, too. The two writers always signed off their letters to each other with the word 'bum'. Larkin and Amis met at the University of Oxford in the early 1940s and became firm friends, united by their sense of humour as well as their literary ambitions. Amis wanted to be a poet but ended up being a novelist, while Larkin, conversely, dreamed of being a great novelist but ended up as a poet.

Philip Larkin's other chief correspondent was Monica Jones, his long-term girlfriend who was a lecturer at nearby Leicester, where they had met in the 1940s when Larkin briefly worked at the library there. Larkin's time at Leicester helped to inspire Amis's most celebrated novel, *Lucky Jim* (1954), whose protagonist, Jim Dixon, was based on Larkin. Larkin's letters to Monica, which were published in 2010, served to reinforce what a big softie Larkin could be: for instance, the fact that he shared with Monica a deep love for the work of Beatrix Potter. And, much as Larkin would sign off his letters to Kingsley Amis with 'bum', he would frequently address Monica, in his letters to her, as Bun – a reference to Beatrix Potter's bunnies.

And although perhaps his most famous poem, 'The Whitsun Weddings', describes a train journey from Hull to London, the actual inspiration for the poem was a journey

Larkin undertook down to Loughborough in August 1956. Hull may have nothing to fear from Loughborough or Leicester so far as 'claims' to Larkin go, but Larkin's time in Leicestershire is often overlooked. Yet it was in Leicestershire that he showed his devotion to his mother, and Leicestershire that introduced him to the woman with whom he would have the most enduring romantic relationship of his life, and which inspired several of his greatest poems.

God's Gift to Coventry

Travelling to Coventry, where Philip Larkin was born in 1922, we find the Godiva Trading Estate, Godiva Place, and even Peeping Tom News. On Broadgate in the city centre stands a bronze statue commemorating Coventry's most famous citizen: she is astride her horse and the plinth quotes lines from Tennyson's 1840 poem 'Godiva', which he composed following a visit to the city. The story of her riding naked through the town is well known: her husband had imposed a heavy tax on the people of Coventry, but promised to abolish it if his wife rode naked through the market. To his surprise, she consented, and after she had performed this unclothed act of equestrianism he had little choice but to lift the tax.

Lady Godiva was a real person, named Godgifu ('god's gift'). She was the wife of Leofric, Earl of Mercia. She's mentioned in the *Domesday Book* and according to the chronicles she died shortly after the Norman Conquest, perhaps in 1067. But Lady Godiva probably never rode naked through the streets of Coventry. For one thing, it wasn't first mentioned until the thirteenth century, nearly two centuries after she died, and then our earliest source for the story is the frequently inaccurate (and endlessly gullible) Roger of Wendover, writing in *Flores Historiarum* (*Flowers of History*), a chronicle that the credulous Roger compiled from hearsay he had picked up from other monks.

Peeping Tom, meanwhile, doesn't turn up until the

eighteenth century, some 700 years after the supposed event took place, and he was likewise a literary invention. (A collection of ballads published in 1778 refers to the Peeper in the prefatory note, but the ballad itself, which is older, makes no mention of him.) The idea is that Tom the tailor, who defied the lady's orders and copped a sneaky peek at her as she rode past, was struck blind for his boldness. This has the ring of legend about it, suggesting the classical story of Actaeon (who was turned into a stag and torn apart by his own hounds for daring to catch a glimpse of the naked goddess Diana while she bathed). And as the Victorians liked to claim, men who spent too much time thinking about, or looking at, naked ladies would be punished with blindness, if they did it enough.

If the Lady Godiva myth is too familiar for you, Warwickshire boasts a number of other fine legends which aren't as well known, but perhaps should be. These include the exploits of Guy of Warwick, a heroic knight who fought in the Crusades and battled dragons, giants, boars, and even, for a bit of variety, a dun cow. You can see Sir Guy's sword at Warwick Castle, which also boasts a fourteenth-century tower named in his honour. The literary associations with Guy of Warwick are more interesting, too: he was the subject of an Elizabethan play of unknown authorship, but possibly written by Shakespeare's contemporary, Ben Jonson. The play is unknown to virtually anyone who isn't a Ben Jonson scholar, which is a shame, as it contains what is perhaps the very first lampoon of William Shakespeare, in the form of a comical character named Philip Sparrow, Guy's sidekick in the play. Like the Bard, Philip Sparrow hails from Stratford-upon-Avon — which is where we are headed . . . in a moment.

Warwickshire . . . Somewhere

Who is being described here? A provincial lad from Warwickshire in England, this poet and dramatist left the sticks for London, where he performed at the royal court, writing and acting in his own plays, including at the court of Queen Elizabeth I. No, not William Shakespeare, but . . . John Heywood.

John Heywood entertained the courts of four English monarchs. Born in Warwickshire (probably in Coventry, though we can't be sure) in around 1497, he played to members of the royal court under Henry VIII, Edward VI, Mary I, and Elizabeth I. However, he ended up fleeing England just six years into Elizabeth's reign, in 1564 – the year that another provincial Warwickshire poet and dramatist was born – when the Act of Uniformity against Catholics was passed. He died in exile in Mechelen, Belgium, in around 1580.

Heywood's links with other literary men were impressive. His father-in-law, John Rastell, was the first printer to publish plays in England. Heywood was related to both Sir Thomas More and John Donne, the latter of whom was Heywood's grandson. Heywood's son Jasper was also a noted poet and translator. Writing was in the Heywood genes.

Unfortunately, so was a bit of mischievousness. Heywood, a staunch Catholic, was nearly hanged for conspiring against the Archbishop of Canterbury, Thomas Cranmer, when he accused Cranmer of heresy in 1543. He was lucky to escape with his life: Sir John Harington, who would later attain fame as the inventor of the flush toilet, recorded that Heywood 'escaped hanging with his mirth', though whether he was actually reprieved on his way to the gallows by regaling the crowd with a few gags is, I'd say, doubtful.

What of his writing, then? Heywood's poetry is not widely read (or even known about) now, but one standout work is 'The Quiet Neighbour', a paean to good neighbours who, though they live next to you, 'wall to wall', are never heard. But his finest legacy is his pioneering work for the English stage, some half a century before the golden age of Elizabethan theatre when William Shakespeare, Christopher Marlowe, Ben Jonson, and Thomas Kyd were all penning plays. Heywood wrote plays for the court from the early 1530s onwards, including *The Play of the Wether*; *The Mery Play betwene Johan Johan, the Husbande, Tyb, his Wyf, and Syr Johan, the Preest*; and *The Play called the foure PP; a newe and a very mery interlude of a palmer, a pardoner, a potycary, a pedler*. But Heywood was also a composer and musician, much praised during his own lifetime, though sadly none of his compositions have survived. As if all that wasn't enough, he even wrote a book of proverbs, including the now well-known sayings 'Out of sight, out of mind', 'Two heads are better than one', and – to complete the Shakespeare connection – 'All's well that ends well'.

The Woman from Stratford

Finally, we arrive in Shakespeare country! The literary significance of Stratford-upon-Avon goes without saying, unless you're an Oxfordian or a Baconian or one of the other naysayers who maintain that the man from Stratford couldn't possibly have written the plays attributed to William Shakespeare. And the fact is that the evidence that 'Shakespeare' and 'the man from Stratford' were one and the same man is overwhelming.

Shakespeare attended a grammar school where he would have studied a range of classical writers, including Ovid, whose work would have a profound influence on his plays and narrative poems. He didn't go to Oxford or Cambridge, but then neither did his contemporaries Ben Jonson, Thomas Kyd, or John Webster, and their plays are shot through with classical allusions and learned literary and historical references. The fact that he 'only' went to school would not have barred him from a career on the London stage, though it's true that he faced some class snobbery from the 'Cambridge wits' when he first arrived in London – most notably Robert Greene, who branded him an 'upstart crow'.

Tourism has been a big part of Stratford for centuries, with many admirers coming from all over the country, and beyond, to pay homage to the nation's poet. Indeed, Shakespeare's home in the town, New Place, was torn down in the eighteenth century by the Reverend Francis

Gastrell because he was getting fed up with all of the visitors showing up to see the house. Sir Walter Scott made his pilgrimage in April 1828, recording in his journal that he 'visited the tomb of the mighty wizard', which he found to be 'in the bad taste of James the First's reign', although he acknowledged that Stratford possessed a certain 'magic'.

But Shakespeare is not the only literary figure to have a strong connection with Stratford. In the late nineteenth century another writer made her home there, and she was the publishing sensation of the age. She also became something of a thorn in the side of local councillors, through her tireless efforts to preserve Stratford as Shakespeare's home town and a piece of English literary history. Although she was born Mary Mackay and would show early promise as a musician (with her talents being encouraged by her parents' neighbour, the novelist and poet George Meredith), she would attain international renown – and notoriety – as Marie Corelli.

To say that Corelli was a popular writer is, remarkably, to play down just how successful she was. Her books sold millions of copies, but more than that, she outsold all of her contemporaries by a clear margin. Her admirers included Winston Churchill, William Ewart Gladstone, and numerous members of the British royal family; Queen Victoria even once remarked that Corelli's novels would still be read once Dickens and George Eliot were forgotten, which shows how dangerous it is to let monarchs try their hands at literary criticism. When her fellow Victorian novelist (and Warwickshire resident) George Eliot received £10,000 for her novel *Romola*, such an amount of money for a publishing advance was unprecedented; by 1901 it's thought Corelli was earning £10,000 for every one of her novels – well over half a million pounds in today's money. Her 1906 novel *Treasures of Heaven* certainly brought her worldly treasures: it sold 100,000 copies on its day of publication alone.

Corelli's rise to hitherto unseen heights of literary stardom had all begun with a faintly ridiculous work of science fiction tinged with supernatural New Age mysticism, *A Romance of Two Worlds*, in 1886, which made her an overnight hit and brought her the admiration of Oscar Wilde. She followed this up with a string of successful novels, including *Thelma* the following year, a book which even popularised the title character's name (derived from an 1840s Swedish novel by Emilie Flygare-Carlén) among English readers. Her most enduring book is *The Sorrows of Satan* (1895), a Faustian novel whose sales, according to Teresa Ransom in *The Amazing Miss Marie Corelli*, outstripped those of all previous novels published in English. Yet who now reads Marie Corelli?

Corelli and her lifelong companion Bertha Vyver (the two were probably lovers though this is largely a matter of speculation) lived at Mason Croft in Stratford from 1901 until Corelli's death in 1924. Corelli's eccentricities – which included having a Venetian gondola shipped over from Italy, complete with a gondolier who was employed to row her up and down the Avon – were well noted by her neighbours, but in 1917 her national reputation was to be destroyed when she was found to have illegally hoarded sugar. The press made her a hate figure, and her books – which were not selling as they once had – would never be read in huge numbers again. And that was the end of the popularity of the most successful novelist of the age.

But when she wasn't being rowed up and down the

Avon in her gondola, Corelli was annoying the residents of Stratford with some altogether more charitable activities, for which we all owe her a debt of gratitude. In 1900, she learned that Sir Theodore Martin intended to obscure the bust of Shakespeare in Holy Trinity Church by erecting a memorial to his wife. Corelli campaigned against this act of 'vandalism', arousing the ire of the *Daily Mail*, which branded her objections as shrieking; Corelli's response was to remark that a shriek is generally more satisfactory than a snuffle, and more effective at getting people's attention.

Mason Croft is now the home of the Shakespeare Institute – and before we leave Stratford behind, it's worth mentioning the persistent myth that Shakespeare died following a particularly heavy drinking binge with his fellow playwrights. The story goes that Shakespeare developed a fever shortly after a heavy boozing session with Ben Jonson and Michael Drayton (a fellow Warwickshire lad) in Stratford-upon-Avon, and that he dropped down and died as a result. This story appears doubtful. Yet we will keep the pub firmly in mind as we move south from Stratford to Oxford.

The Bird and Baby of Oxford

The seventeenth-century biographer and antiquarian John Aubrey claimed that Shakespeare, when on his way home to Stratford from London, stopped off at the Crown tavern (since destroyed) on Cornmarket in Oxford. The proprietors of the Crown were John and Jane Davenant, and their son, William – who would himself go on to be a poet and playwright – was, Aubrey tells us, Shakespeare's godson. Or, if you believe the gossip (and Aubrey usually did), Shakespeare's biological son.

Although the Crown is no more, Oxford is full of fine pubs with strong literary associations. Matthew Arnold memorably described Oxford as the 'sweet city with her dreaming spires' in his poem 'Thyrsis', but its taverns are where we find the juiciest literary links. If you're in Oxford and have half an hour to spare, pop into the Eagle and Child ('Bird and Baby') on St Giles' and have a drink in the back room – known as the Rabbit Room – where C. S. Lewis, J. R. R. Tolkien, and other members of the Inklings used to meet on Tuesday lunchtimes from the 1930s until the 1960s to discuss their writing. In the 1950s, it was in the Eagle and Child that self-confessed Tolkien fanatic Christopher Lee, who reread *The Lord of the Rings* every year and would later play Saruman in the film adaptation, met his literary hero by chance one day. Lee described how, when Tolkien walked in, he nearly fell off his chair in surprise.

The Eagle and Child wasn't the only Oxford pub the Inklings frequented for their meetings, though it's the best known. (They were also fond of the Lamb and Flag across the road.) Nor did Tolkien and Lewis found the Inklings: it was an undergraduate named Edward Tangye Lean who established a group of that name, with the intention of bringing writers together to discuss compositions they were working on, in the early 1930s. Tolkien and Lewis attended the meetings, and after Lean graduated, they co-opted the name for their own 'club', meeting regularly to discuss their fantasy writing.

Lewis's love of fantasy and world-building began at a young age: as children, he and his elder brother created the fictional world of Boxen, a box world which featured talking animals including King Bunny – quite fitting for an author who would, as an adult, meet to discuss his writing in a place known as the Rabbit Room. (The fact that his brother was named Warren only intensifies the rabbit theme.)

The Inklings were an odd bunch with a puckish sense of humour. According to Tolkien's biographer Humphrey Carpenter, Tolkien and Lewis once attended a New Year's Eve party dressed up as polar bears, which would have been more understandable if they'd been going to a fancy-dress party, but they weren't. The sight of Tolkien wearing a sheepskin and with his face painted white is somewhat at odds with the donnish pipe-smoking image that people tend to associate with the author of *The Hobbit*. (Carpenter also reveals that Tolkien was known to dress up as an axe-wielding Anglo-Saxon warrior and chase his bewildered neighbour down the road. No wonder he eventually had to leave Oxford.)

Students recalled Tolkien's eccentricity, as Philip and Carol Zaleski reveal in *The Fellowship: The Literary Lives of the Inklings*. An undergraduate once asked him whether he thought there was any factual basis to the legends of dragons and other mythical beings, only to watch in astonishment as Tolkien dug around in his pockets, producing a tiny green shoe which he declared, with apparent sincerity, to have belonged to a leprechaun. Lewis, too, was something of an eccentric, for all his donnish seriousness and his reputation as a leading Christian apologist and literary critic. Alastair Fowler recalled that Lewis, who was his tutor at Oxford, sometimes broke off a doctoral supervision to pop next door and urinate noisily into a chamber pot, all the while carrying on the flow of conversation through the door.

This sense of quirkiness also found its way into the Inklings' meetings, which regularly involved members of the group competing to see who could read the work of Irish novelist Amanda McKittrick Ros – according to some critics, the worst writer ever to have found her way into print – for the longest without laughing.

Binsey Treacle Mine

To most poetry lovers, the village of Binsey immediately evokes the 'Binsey Poplars' immortalised in Gerard Manley Hopkins's poem. Hopkins wrote his poem in 1879 shortly after he'd revisited the small hamlet of Godstow near Oxford, a few miles north of Binsey, to find that 'the aspens that lined the river [Thames] are everyone felled'. His sadness and anger inspired the opening lines:

> My aspens dear, whose airy cages quelled,
> Quelled or quenched in leaves the leaping sun,
> All felled, felled, are all felled;

But it turns out that Binsey has a fair bit more literary significance than a group of trees. It is also the location of St Frideswide's Well, which is thought to have been the inspiration for the treacle well mentioned by the Dormouse in *Alice's Adventures in Wonderland* (1865). Charles Lutwidge Dodgson, better known as Lewis Carroll, was the original 'Oxford scholar who was also a fantasy-author', nearly a century before Tolkien and Lewis. He used to visit Binsey, and several biographers have speculated that the real-life inspiration for the character of Alice, Alice Liddell, may have accompanied him. Alice's nurse, who bore the rather wonderfully Dickensian name of Miss Prickett, came from Binsey.

The local name for the well was the Binsey treacle mine,

as in the original meaning of the word 'treacle' – a curative fluid or medicine. But the old joke that treacle could be mined like coal was doing the rounds by the mid nineteenth century, and was the equivalent of the 1950s *Panorama* April Fools' Day prank involving the spaghetti tree, or cheerily enquiring of someone whether they are aware that the word 'gullible' has been removed from the dictionary.

Then another fantasy novelist, Terry Pratchett, picked up the joke, having possibly encountered it in Carroll's book, and created Treacle Mine Road, one of the streets in the city Ankh-Morpork in his *Discworld* novels.

Treacle Mine Road remained the stuff of fantasy, until a fan of Pratchett's work campaigned to have his local Somerset town, Wincanton, twinned with Ankh-Morpork. The proposal was approved and in 2009 one of the new streets on a housing development in Wincanton was named Treacle Mine Road in honour of Pratchett's fictional street.

Dr Fell of Longworth

A mile or so north of the wonderfully named village of Kingston Bagpuize – home of Kingston Bagpuize House, where the son of *The Thirty-Nine Steps* author John Buchan lived – you'll find Longworth, the birthplace of John Fell (1625–86), who was Dean of Christ Church, Oxford – the same post that Henry Liddell, father of Carroll's muse Alice, would occupy two centuries later.

The reputation of Oxford had been severely damaged by Cromwell and the Parliamentarians during the English Civil War. As Dean of Christ Church and, later, Vice Chancellor of the University of Oxford and, later still, Bishop of Oxford, Fell appears to have done a great deal for the city, paying for the repair of a number of local churches out of his own pocket and installing the famous bell, Great Tom, in the clock tower of Christ Church. He was also instrumental in reforming Oxford University Press, which had been printing books for nearly two centuries but had never officially been established as a publisher. In his service to the Press, Fell acquired a large stock of typographical punches and matrices from the Netherlands, now known as the Fell Types. He persuaded Gilbert Sheldon to let the new theatre that had just been built in his honour, the Sheldonian, be used as headquarters for the Press, and in 1674 he began publishing the *Oxford Almanack*, an annual calendar which is still published today.

Yet few people outside of Oxford – or outside the world

of typography – will have heard of John Fell. Well, that's not quite true. His name lives on in the four-line rhyme that one of his students, Tom Brown, wrote about him:

> I do not like thee, Dr Fell,
> The reason why I cannot tell;
> But this I know, and know full well,
> I do not like thee, Dr Fell.

And so a great benefactor to the city and university of Oxford came to be a byword for someone towards whom one feels an irrational aversion. Fittingly, nobody knows why Brown took such a dislike to Fell, but one (probably apocryphal) story relates how Fell had threatened Brown with expulsion for misconduct, but promised he would revoke the sentence if Brown could translate some lines from the Roman poet Martial, whereupon (the too good to be true story goes) Brown came up with the lines quoted above. There are several reasons to doubt this tale, but at any rate, Brown's poem was not altogether original: Thomas Forde's 1660 poem *Faenestra in Pectore* contains a strikingly similar quatrain which runs, 'I love thee not Nel / But why, I can't tell: / But this I can tell, / I love thee not Nel.'

Brown ended up leaving Oxford without a degree, but with his place in countless poetry anthologies assured thanks to this single plagiarised four-line verse, and Fell, who had done so much for Oxford University Press and for the city of Oxford in general, would have to settle for having his name used as the shorthand for inexplicable dislike.

Britannia of Cliveden

Given how ubiquitous it is at sports ceremonies and royal occasions, it really is surprising to reflect that nobody really knows where the British national anthem came from.

The music is popularly attributed to Thomas Arne (1710–78), the composer also responsible for 'A-Hunting We Will Go', but as Percy Scholes has pointed out in *The Oxford Companion to Music*, the tune of 'God Save the Queen' is strikingly similar to earlier songs from the sixteenth and seventeenth centuries, including one by a composer with the quintessentially English name of John Bull (*circa* 1562–1628). The truth is that nobody's quite sure who composed the tune. The same goes for the lyrics, including that controversial verse about crushing rebellious Scots. It's been suggested that Henry Carey, the poet who also gave us the phrase 'namby-pamby' (in his lampooning of the babyish verses of his contemporary, Ambrose Philips), was responsible for them, but this, too, is something of a guess.

What's more, despite the popular belief that 'God Save the Queen' is the official national anthem of the United Kingdom, it's never been officially proclaimed as such and has simply attained its exalted status through general custom and tradition. A song based around the phrase 'God save the king' has been sung at every coronation since 973, so time, not official decree, has bestowed upon it the status it – rightly or wrongly – enjoys.

Thomas Arne, who often gets the credit for the tune of 'God Save the Queen', definitely *did* compose the music for 'Rule, Britannia'. Unlike 'God Save the Queen', this other famous patriotic anthem has a clear origin, which can be traced to a specific date, 1 August 1740, when the song was first performed at Cliveden, the royal residence of Frederick, Prince of Wales, in Buckinghamshire. Letters discovered by the Oxford historian Oliver Cox in 2012 suggest that the song was written as an attack on the king, George II, and his prime minister, Robert Walpole. (The Prince had drifted apart from his father and formed a rival faction, members of whom had gathered at Cliveden on that August day to hear 'Rule, Britannia'.) It's certainly telling that the modern lyrics to 'God Save the King' were produced shortly after this.

'Rule, Britannia' formed the musical finale of a masque about Alfred the Great, with none too subtle parallels drawn between Alfred the heroic Saxon king (and putative founder of England's navy) and Frederick the ambitious prince, who was keen on expanding Britain's naval power. The lyrics were written by James Thomson, the Scottish poet whose long poem *The Seasons* had already brought him considerable fame and fortune.

However we feel about 'Rule, Britannia' as a patriotic anthem – and it's worth reflecting that at the same time Frederick and his cronies were enthusiastically bellowing that Britain never will be slaves, the Brits were busy enslaving much of the rest of the world – one thing is clear: most of us get the words wrong. In Thomson's lyrics, the word 'never' appears only once in the line 'Britain never will be slaves', yet despite this it is almost universally sung with three 'nevers', as though the nation has collectively developed a stammer. Similarly, the second line is 'Britannia, rule the waves' (as in a command) yet it is commonly misheard and misspoken as 'Britannia *rules* the waves'. There, glad we've got that cleared up.

The eighteenth century was the golden age of British anthems and hymns. As well as the official version of 'God Save the King' and 'Rule, Britannia', we also got the *Olney Hymns*, the most famous of which was 'Amazing Grace', composed at the small village of Olney (also, as it happens, in Buckinghamshire) by William Cowper and John Newton. Just south of Olney, you find the new town of Milton Keynes, and to the south of Milton Keynes, our next stop – Bletchley.

Bletchley's Major Claim to Fame

As you enter the town of Bletchley, you'll notice a series of signs announcing that you are entering the 'Home of the Codebreakers'. The codebreakers who worked at Bletchley Park during the Second World War, toiling away in secret and being sworn to silence for many years after the end of the conflict, are thought to have helped to shorten the war by two years.

As well as the genius of Alan Turing, a number of poets were drafted in to undertake important codebreaking work at Bletchley – though not in order to compose verses to bamboozle German airmen. They were simply exceptionally intelligent individuals who happened to write poetry. These included Angus Wilson, Vernon Watkins (who met his future wife, Gwen, there), F. T. Prince (who met his future wife, Elizabeth, there), and Henry Reed, who wrote his most famous poem, 'The Naming of Parts', while working at Bletchley Park. Philip Larkin applied to do war work at Bletchley, but was turned down. Patrick Wilkinson wrote an epic poem about the codebreakers, 'The Other Side', which he composed during a blackout on the train to Cambridge; unfortunately, the poem has never been published.

But there is another literary link with the wartime codebreakers at Bletchley Park – indeed, a link with the most popular novelist of the age. How did Bletchley Park lead to Agatha Christie being briefly investigated by MI5? All because one of her novels, *N or M?* (1941), featured a character named Major Bletchley. Most of the world had no idea that Bletchley was the site where some of the most ingenious minds had gathered, but British Intelligence was understandably concerned to see such a suggestive and unusual name – suggestive to those in the know, at least – featuring in a popular author's work. When you add into the mix a wartime storyline focusing on the search for German traitors, and two protagonists, Tommy and Tuppence Beresford, who had previously worked for British Intelligence, things started to look more than a little bit suspicious. It didn't help that the aforementioned Major Bletchley claims to know crucial British wartime secrets.

When the MI5 operatives heading the investigation discovered that one of Bletchley Park's codebreakers, Alfred Dillwyn 'Dilly' Knox, was actually a good friend of Agatha Christie's, it must've started to look as though the queen of detective fiction was going to end up starring in something more closely resembling a Graham Greene novel than one of her own books. Could Knox have been sharing Bletchley Park's secrets with the novelist? He unequivocally denied it, and agreed to speak to Christie to find out how much, if anything, the popular author really did know.

Knox, and MI5, were gratified – and, one suspects, more than a little relieved – when they received the solution to this real-life mystery. Christie informed her friend that, having once been stuck at Bletchley railway station on her way from Oxford to London, she had decided to take 'revenge' on the town by giving the name to one of her least lovable characters. The Bletchley codebreakers' true role as the intellectual saviours of the war would not emerge until the 1970s.

A Cottage in Chalfont St Giles

Milton Keynes, which we've just left behind, was *not* named after John Milton (or after the economist, John Maynard Keynes), but after a medieval village of that name which forms part of the new town. But there *is* a Buckinghamshire connection to John Milton, and it can be found on the outskirts of the Chilterns where you'll find the charming little village of Chalfont St Giles, where Milton (1608–74) completed his epic 1667 poem *Paradise Lost*. It was the work of many years, but the small rural cottage where he finished the poem has become a sort of shrine – and site of pilgrimage – for Milton admirers and people who like having a look round sixteenth-century thatched cottages.

It was, it's safe to say, a long road to Chalfont St Giles and *Paradise Lost*. Milton only came to the village in 1665 because bubonic plague forced him out of his home town of London and into the provinces. And Milton was a Londoner born and bred: born, in fact, in Bread Street, the same street where his fellow poet John Donne had been born several decades earlier. As a teenager, Milton began writing an epic poem in Latin about the Gunpowder Plot. He left the work, *in quintum novembris* (remember, remember . . .), unfinished, but this early attempt at an epic poem shows how gradually the idea of *Paradise Lost* had gestated over a period of some forty years. In this abandoned Latin epic, as Stuart Kelly observes in his endlessly informative *The Book of Lost Books*, it is Satan –

the villain (or should that be antihero?) of *Paradise Lost* – who suggests the idea of the Gunpowder Plot to the Pope, who then enlists the help of Robert Catesby, Guy Fawkes, and the others. So from an early age, Satan was on Milton's mind as a suitable character for an epic.

Milton's piece of Latin juvenilia remained unfinished, as did his next attempt, a poem – this time in English – about King Arthur. In fact, he never got around to starting, let alone finishing, the poem – it never left the planning stage. For one thing, his other work kept him busy, travelling around Europe engaged on diplomatic missions. In 1638, while in Florence, he even met Galileo, an encounter which he recorded in his 1644 pamphlet *Areopagitica*, one of the greatest defences of freedom of the press in all of English literature. Then, to make the writing process that much more difficult, in 1652 Milton became completely blind, and had to dictate *Paradise Lost* to a string of secretaries, including his daughters.

It would be *Paradise Lost* that allowed Milton to flex his epic poetry muscles and show what they were capable of. Many people have an idea of the poem as a po-faced religious epic about temptation, sin, evil, and a loss of innocence – the poem does, after all, retell the Fall of Man from the Book of Genesis – yet it also features all sorts of weird and surprising details. Among the oddest descriptions is the following passage:

> Tasting concoct, digest, assimilate,
> And corporeal to incorporeal turn.

This is, essentially, a description of angels farting.

Milton lived in the cottage that bears his name for less

than a year, yet it has become *the* residence most closely associated with him, by default more than anything else – it's the only one of his houses still standing. Thomas Ellwood, Milton's friend who hired the cottage for him in 1665, called it 'that pretty box in St Giles'. It is open to the public, so you can judge its prettiness for yourself.

Stoke Poges, Buckinghamshire

There was a time when pretty much every schoolchild could quote lines from Thomas Gray's poem 'Elegy Written in a Country Churchyard', so widely was it taught in Britain. And it's an endlessly quotable poem: Gray's 'Elegy' gave Thomas Hardy the phrase 'far from the madding crowd', which he used as the title of his fourth published novel; the phrase 'paths of glory' was used as the title for Stanley Kubrick's 1957 anti-war film; and 'mute inglorious Milton' has become well known as a reference to the might-have-beens who lived their lives in quiet obscurity in country parishes, lacking the means and education – which, despite all his subsequent setbacks, Milton nevertheless enjoyed – to achieve greatness.

Gray completed 'Elegy in a Country Churchyard' in 1750 and sent the poem to his friend Horace Walpole (the author of the first Gothic novel, *The Castle of Otranto*, and coiner of the word 'serendipity'), who circulated it among his literary friends before Gray published the poem on 15 February 1751, one day before a pirated edition was due to be published without Gray's permission. This is the only reason Gray agreed to let the poem appear in print in the first place.

But the germ of the poem actually goes back to 1742, when the young poet Richard West – a friend of both Gray and Walpole – died while only in his mid twenties. Gray wrote a sonnet on the death of his friend, but it would be the 'Elegy Written in a Country Churchyard' – a poem lamenting not just West but all such folk who died in obscurity – that would prove his lasting legacy. (In the same year that West died, Gray coined the nonce word 'leucocholy', for 'a white Melancholy' which 'though it seldom laughs or dances, nor ever amounts to what one calls Joy or Pleasure, yet is a good easy sort of a state'. 'Melancholy', meanwhile, is from the Greek for 'black bile'.)

Despite its reputation as one of the most famous elegies in English poetry, Gray's 'Elegy' is not strictly an elegy at all. It doesn't mourn West or any other single individual, but is instead more of an ode, which sees Gray meditating on death and the lives of simple rustic folk. (Confusingly, although Gray's 'Elegy' isn't an elegy in the strictest sense but more of an ode, his other most famous poem, 'Ode on the Death of a Favourite Cat, Drowned in a Tub of Goldfishes', written about the death of Walpole's pet, is more of an elegy than an ode. Titles of eighteenth-century poems, it seems, can be misleading things.) Nor was it written in a country churchyard: the place referred to in the poem's title belonged to St Giles' parish church at Stoke Poges, but it's likely that Gray had written much of the poem before he moved to Stoke Poges. At best, then, it's an 'Ode Completed in a Country Churchyard'. But admittedly that lacks a certain emotional punch.

Old Etonians

Thomas Gray captured the blissful ignorance of young Etonians in his 'Ode on a Distant Prospect of Eton College' – which is, actually, an ode, proving he could occasionally use titles responsibly.

Many famous writers have been educated at Eton over the centuries: as well as Thomas Gray and his friend Horace Walpole, the long list of illustrious alumni includes George Orwell, Ian Fleming, Henry Fielding, Algernon Charles Swinburne, M. R. James, Robert Bridges, Aldous Huxley, and Anthony Powell. But perhaps the Old Etonian who passed the most curious time at Eton was the Romantic poet and advocate of free love, Percy Bysshe Shelley (1792–1822).

Shelley initially disliked his time at Eton with a passion, and especially hated the culture of fagging, which involves junior boys acting as, effectively, servants for older students. Yet his years at Eton were productive. He published a Gothic novel, *Zastrozzi*, and wrote a second, *St Irvyne*, which appeared shortly after he left the school in 1810. He translated half of Pliny the Elder's multi-volume *Natural History* from the original Latin. But not all of his activities showed him in quite so studious a mode. He was accused of hiding a bulldog in his teacher's desk and once blew up a tree in his school's grounds. (Indeed, blowing things up seems to have been a favourite hobby since Shelley had been at prep school, where he'd experimented with gunpowder whenever he could get hold of it, and once blew the lid off his desk during a lesson.) William Cory, who was later assistant master at Eton, recalled how Edward Coleridge (nephew of the poet Samuel Taylor Coleridge) showed him the tree that Shelley had blown up with gunpowder, with Coleridge adding, 'that was his last bit of naughtiness at school'. Coleridge also told Cory that 'Shelley-baiting' was a more or less daily occurrence during the future poet's early time at the school. Quite why he was seized upon in this way is not entirely clear.

Things might have remained so, but Shelley does appear to have got his act together. He didn't take to the head-master of Eton, a strict disciplinarian with the name John Keate (so near, and yet so far, from Shelley's fellow Romantic poet John Keats), though he admired Dr James Lind, a Scottish physician and co-founder of the Royal Society of Edinburgh, who took the young poet under his wing. This helped to make Shelley's final year at Eton more bearable, even enjoyable. He would go from Eton to the University of Oxford, though he would be sent down in his first year for writing a pamphlet, *The Necessity of Atheism*, which further demonstrated Shelley's free-thinking spirit and rejection of traditional authority.

Lost in Windsor

One of Henry James's shorter novels, *The Aspern Papers* (1888), is based on the letters Percy Bysshe Shelley wrote to Mary Shelley's stepsister, Claire Clairmont. Which is as good a reason as any to skip from Eton College to nearby Windsor, and to listen in on the US-born English writer Henry James (1843–1916) asking for directions.

Henry James's literary style is marked by wordiness, circumlocution, and very long sentences. As Mrs Henry Adams pithily put it, Henry James chews more than he bites off. Or as H. G. Wells mocked his contemporary, a Henry James novel 'is like a church lit but without a congregation to distract you, with every light and line focused on the high altar. And on the altar, very reverently placed, intensely there, is a dead kitten, an egg-shell, a bit of string.'

It turns out that this wasn't literary affectation: Henry James actually talked the way he wrote. When he and his friend Edith Wharton arrived in Windsor one rainy evening, in Wharton's motorcar, they lost their way. James decided to ask a passing pedestrian, a doddering old man, the way to King's Road:

> My friend, to put it to you in two words, this lady and I have just arrived here from Slough; that is to say, to be more strictly accurate, we have recently passed through Slough on our way here, having actually motored to

Windsor from Rye, which was our point of departure; and the darkness having overtaken us, we should be much obliged if you would tell us where we now are in relation, say, to the High Street, which, as you of course know, leads to the Castle, after leaving on the left hand the turn down to the railway station. In short, in short, my good man, what I want to put to you in a word is this: supposing we have already (as I have reason to think we have) driven past the turn down to the railway station (which, in that case, by the way, would probably not have been on our left hand, but on our right), where are we now in relation to . . .

Wharton, despairing of her friend's hesitancy and indirect manner, told him to cut to the chase and ask the old man the way to King's Road. 'Ye're in it,' the man replied.

Dark and Stormy at Knebworth

A mile or so to the south-west of Stevenage in Hertfordshire, you'll find Knebworth House, home of the Lytton family since the fifteenth century. In literary circles, the most famous Lytton is Sir Edward Bulwer Lytton (1803–73), or, to give him his full name, Edward George Earle Lytton Bulwer Lytton, 1st Baron Lytton, which should be enough Lyttons for anyone to be getting on with.

Having said that, and despite often being known as Bulwer-Lytton, most biographers refer to him as Bulwer, since he seems to have changed his name about as frequently as his socks. But then, the number of people who know his name at all is now not that large. This is surprising when we consider that, for a while during the 1820s and 1830s, he was the most popular novelist in Britain. He'd begun his writing career at a young age writing derivative poetry heavily influenced by Byron: his first volume, *Ismael*, was published by Hatchards at his mother's expense when Lytton was just sixteen. His adulation of Byron even extended to exchanging intimate letters with, and allowing himself to be seduced by, Byron's former lover, Lady Caroline Lamb, who lived nearby at Brocket Hall.

But it was his novels that made Lytton successful and very rich. It's hard to think of a novelist who has left more of a mark on all sorts of aspects of our daily lives yet whose work has suffered such a sharp decline in popularity. It wasn't always this way. In fact, his work was so popular it left lasting legacies on everything from everyday phrases (he coined the saying 'The pen is mightier than the sword' in his 1839 play *Richelieu*, and was also the originator of the expression 'the great unwashed') to the way men dress. This latter feat was achieved as a result of his first successful novel *Pelham* (1828), a 'silver fork' novel about upper-class fashionable society, published when Bulwer was still only in his mid twenties. Prior to his novel, the colour of smart evening dress for men could be any colour; Bulwer changed that. As his biographer T. H. S. Escott put it, *Pelham* 'caused the black swallow-tail coat to become compulsory for evening wear'. It has remained so ever since.

Despite this, his novels are no longer popular, and you only have to open one, more or less at random, to see why. Feast your eyes upon this passage, for instance, from his 1829 novel *Devereux*, in which the narrator apostrophises the nearby brook:

'Wild brooklet,' I cried, as my thoughts rushed into words, 'fret on, our lot is no longer the same; your wanderings and your murmurs are wasted in solitude and shade; your voice dies and re-awakes, but without an echo; your waves spread around their path neither fertility nor terror; their anger is idle, and their freshness is lavished on a sterile soil; the sun shines in vain for you, through these unvarying wastes of silence and gloom; Fortune freights not your channel with her hoarded stores, and Pleasure ventures not her silken sails upon your tide; not even the solitary idler roves beside you, to consecrate with human fellowship your melancholy course; no shape of beauty bends over your turbid waters, or mirrors in your breast the loveliness that hallows earth.'

Henry James, then, wasn't the first to write such long, meandering sentences. The novel's no longer in print, but if that's whetted (or wetted) your appetite for more, this hydrophilic encomium runs on for a fair bit longer, and can be found online.

It is easy to scoff, but Bulwer's readers lapped this stuff up, and as late as 1857 he was still the most requested author at W. H. Smith's railway station bookstalls. Even in his later years the only novelist who outsold him was Dickens, with whom Bulwer became friends. The two authors acted together in Ben Jonson's *Every Man in his Humour* at Knebworth in 1850. It was Bulwer who convinced Dickens to alter the ending of *Great Expectations* and to give his eager public the happy (or at least less doom-laden) conclusion Dickens had originally planned, where Pip and Estella are not reunited. What's more, Dickens borrowed (if that is quite the word) the ending of Bulwer's French Revolution novel *Zanoni*, in which a man takes the place of someone else at the guillotine, for his own *A Tale of Two Cities*.

Bulwer was also pals with the novelist and prime minister Benjamin Disraeli, who modelled the character of the Honourable Bertie Tremaine in *Endymion* (1880) on his friend. Such were Lytton's political connections, in fact, that in 1862 he was offered the throne of Greece, which he declined, preferring the 'calm Academe of Knebworth'.

However, his life wasn't all hobnobbing with the great and good of Victorian England. In 1858, while he was standing as a parliamentary candidate for Hertfordshire, his wife Rosina – from whom he had by then formally separated – showed up at the hustings and publicly denounced him, citing her husband's numerous infidelities and blaming him for their daughter's death from typhus, claiming his neglect had led to her demise. He responded by having her quietly put away in a mental asylum. (She was released a few weeks later.)

It was at Knebworth House – which he gave a Gothic makeover in the 1850s, installing domes, turrets, and gargoyles – that Bulwer felt most comfortable, and it was here that he wrote an early work of science fiction which deserves to be better known than it is. In *The Coming Race* (1871), the narrator accidentally finds himself in a subterranean utopian world populated by a telepathic people known as the Vril-ya. They power themselves with the help of a life-giving fluid known as vril, whose properties are many and diverse. Some people, including the Theosophists, even thought that vril actually existed. It didn't, but when the makers of a new product, a beef extract they intended to market across Britain, were casting around for a name for their new food, they formed their brand name by blending the word 'bovine' with 'vril', suggesting that this beefy drink had energising properties similar to those provided by Bulwer's fictional elixir. His novel may have sunk into an undeserved obscurity, but this one word from his book can be found on the shelves of every supermarket in the country, its literary legacy unknown to most consumers.

However, much of Bulwer's fiction is not as readable as *The Coming Race*. Indeed, as well as giving us 'The pen is mightier than the sword' he was the first person to use the most famous – or perhaps infamous – opening line in all of fiction. His 1830 novel *Paul Clifford* begins with the immortal words, 'It was a dark and stormy night . . .' The annual Bulwer-Lytton Fiction Contest, a competition sponsored by San José State University in California, aims to find a deliberately bad opening line for a new novel.

As the Bulwer-Lytton Fiction Contest shows, his name has not *quite* been forgotten; but what he'd make of his legacy is difficult to say. Nowadays the estate where he wrote his largely unread books is better known for big rock concerts.

The Book of St Albans

I've often thought that someone should write a book about interesting thirds. Firsts are interesting, of course, and the silver medallists of history have their place, but the third of something is often fascinating in ways that can baffle and surprise.

Take Shakespeare's First Folio, for instance – or rather, don't take that, take his Third Folio instead. Copies of the Third Folio are worth more than a First Folio (which itself sells for a small fortune at auctions), because most of the Third Folios perished in the Great Fire of London. In the confessedly unlikely event that you should find an old Third Folio gathering dust in your attic, don't throw it out thinking collectors are interested only in first editions.

Or consider the third university set up in England, which was in, of all places, Northampton in 1261, when a group of renegade scholars fled Cambridge and received a royal charter to establish a new university. Unfortunately, it only lasted four years before King Henry III changed his mind and ordered its dissolution. (He also decreed that there would never be a university in the town again, so when the modern-day university was established in 2005, they had to overturn a 750-year-old piece of red tape.)

The third printing press in England, too, was something of a curiosity. It was set up at the Abbey Gateway in St Albans in 1479, by a schoolmaster whose name may have been John Haule, though nobody seems sure who he was;

however, aptly, given Haule's profession, the Abbey Gateway now forms part of St Albans School. The St Albans printing press followed hot on the heels of Caxton's Westminster premises set up three years earlier, and the university press created at Oxford in 1478, where the very first book printed, a commentary on the Apostles' Creed, carried a misprint on its title page (it was dated 1468 instead of 1478, which did at least have the effect of making Oxford University Press sound more established than it then was).

The jewel in the crown at the Abbey Gateway printing press was, without doubt, *The Book of Saint Albans* (1486), which was at least partly the work of a prioress named Juliana Berners from the nearby Sopwell Priory. (Her name is sometimes rendered as Julyan Barnes, which makes her sound like the unlikely medieval ancestor of the author of *Flaubert's Parrot*.) According to Alan Tennant in *On the Wing*, this makes Berners 'almost certainly' the first female author of a printed book in English – 'and, until J. K. Rowling, by far the most successful'. Whether Berners was the author of all of the book is difficult to ascertain, but she appears to have contributed at least one-third of it, namely the section on hunting. The other two-thirds cover hawking and heraldry, the latter of these being printed in colour – making *The Book of St Albans* the first printed English book to feature colour printing.

The Book of St Albans remained popular for over a century after that first edition rolled off the new printing press in 1486. A fourth section, covering fishing, was added to a subsequent printing of the book, and appears to be the first book on fly fishing, some five centuries before J. R. Hartley's fictional tome, *Fly-Fishing*. But it is the prioress's section that has probably had the most profound influence, thanks to a jocular glossary of collective nouns which is appended to Berners' chapters on hunting. These include many terms which, as David Crystal argues in *The Story of English in 100 Words*, were probably invented specially for the book: 'an unkindness of ravens' appears to have already been in use, but many of the others, such as 'a diligence of messengers', 'a sentence of judges', 'a nonpatience of wives', 'an abominable sight of monks', and 'a superfluity of nuns' may well have been dreamt up by Berners/Barnes or by her fellow sisters at the priory as a bit of light amusement.

Within fifty years of the publication of *The Book of St Albans*, the 'superfluity of nuns' at the priory – and elsewhere throughout England – would be dealt a deadly blow by Henry VIII and his ministers, who, with the dissolution of the monasteries in the 1530s, put an end to such religious institutions and such high jinks with collective nouns. St Albans Priory would be hit like many others. There would be no more 'abominable sights of monks'.

A Pilgrimage to Bedford Jail

After all that talk of monks and abbeys, how about a quiz about one of the most famous writer-preachers England has ever produced? Well, one quick question at least. Which book did John Bunyan write while he was in Bedford gaol?

The Pilgrim's Progress – Bunyan's 1678 work of Christian allegory which is sometimes called the first English novel – was begun, but probably not completed, while Bunyan was in prison. But he did complete another book while serving a prison sentence: *Grace Abounding to the Chief of Sinners, or The Brief Relation of the Exceeding Mercy of God in Christ to his Poor Servant John Bunyan*, which was published in 1666.

Of course, this is not to deny the importance of *The Pilgrim's Progress* and the extent to which it was influenced by Bedford and its environs. It's one of the biggest-selling books ever written: some estimates put it behind only the Bible in the number of copies sold. By the time Bunyan died just ten years after it was published, there were an estimated 100,000 copies in circulation. Bunyan also wrote a little-known sequel to *The Pilgrim's Progress* – called, perhaps inevitably, *The Pilgrim's Progress II* – in 1684. In the original book, the protagonist, Christian, had left behind his wife and children, and the follow-up focuses on 'Christiana'.

Bedfordshire was central to *The Pilgrim's Progress*. Many of the allegorical places which appear in the book appear to have been based on real locations in the county: the

Slough of Despond, for instance, was modelled on the grey clay deposits around the town of Stewartby, which would later be used in the nearby London Brick works. Similarly, Doubting Castle in the book is based on Ampthill Castle, which unfortunately was dismantled during Bunyan's lifetime – although this is fitting, since Bunyan himself has Doubting Castle destroyed in the book.

Bunyan was born near Harrowden in 1628, and fought during the English Civil War – he was billeted at Newport Pagnell, just outside the modern town of Milton Keynes, where he probably honed the writing skills that would serve him so well in later life. He was nearly shot in the head while on guard duty one night – but fortunately, another soldier had taken his place. (Fortunately for Bunyan, anyway.) This helped to convince Bunyan that he was one of God's elect – the chosen few.

Bunyan's *Grace Abounding* is his autobiography, but Bunyan attracted a number of followers – he was an influential preacher, and it was preaching without a licence that landed him in gaol in the first place – and they, too, sometimes left autobiographical accounts of their dealings with him. The most famous of these is Agnes Beaumont, of Edworth in Bedfordshire, who wrote a short account describing the events surrounding the death of her father in 1674 and her encounters with Bunyan. Accused of having poisoned her father with Bunyan's help, Beaumont faced burning at the stake, had she been found guilty. Luckily for her she wasn't; but one of the things that had helped to drive a rift between her and her father, as she revealed in 'The Narrative of the Persecution of Agnes Beaumont', was the fact that he'd caught her riding off to a church meeting on the back of Bunyan's horse, and was so angered that when she returned home he locked the door and refused to let her back in the house, so Agnes had to pass a freezing night sleeping – or trying to – in the barn. (Agnes didn't mind, because she was filled with pride at riding on the great Bunyan's horse.) And as we're talking of horse-riding, let's venture across to East Anglia – on horseback, of course . . .

Norfolk's Beauty

Norfolk was home to a bestselling nineteenth-century female writer for children. Mrs Sewell's tales sold over a million copies, entertaining countless young readers. Her name was Mary Sewell, but despite her extraordinary popularity during her lifetime, posterity would see her name eclipsed by a more famous Sewell – her own daughter, Anna.

Anna Sewell's novel *Black Beauty* is one of the biggest-selling novels of all time. Published in 1877, it was a huge success from the start. Although Sewell died five months after the book appeared (the cause of her death has been attributed variously to tuberculosis and hepatitis), she lived long enough to learn that she had written a bestseller. And 'bestseller' is certainly the word to describe *Black Beauty*: it has sold over 50 million copies in total. When it appeared in a (pirated) edition in America in 1890, it broke publishing records. According to Melissa Holbrook Pierson in *Dark Horses and Black Beauties*, it's the sixth biggest-selling English-language book of all time. Sewell was paid twenty pounds for the book.

It was her only novel. She died in 1878 (she is buried in the Quaker cemetery in Lamas, Norfolk) but had been lame and confined to the family home for much of her life after injuring her ankles when she slipped and fell while walking home from school in the rain. She was born and died in Norfolk, and although she lived in various other parts of the country, Norfolk was her home in her final years, when she began working on her novel.

Black Beauty is described on its title page as 'translated from the original equine'. Sewell's unusual conceit was to tell the story from the perspective of the horse rather than use a human or impersonal 'omniscient' narrator. This makes it the ancestor of – and a possible influence on – some notable later animal-narrated stories, such as Rudyard Kipling's 'The Maltese Cat' (1895), which centres on a polo match told from the perspective of the ponies.

And although the book is now one of the classic children's novels in the language, Sewell wrote it not with children in mind, but rather specifically for people who worked with horses, the animals which, in her invalid state, she increasingly relied on. The book's 'special aim', she wrote, was 'to induce kindness, sympathy, and an understanding treatment of horses'.

Writing was in the Sewell blood, and Sewell's mother, Mary Wright Sewell (1797–1884), who survived her daughter by six years, wrote a number of bestsellers. Among her biggest-selling works was the sentimental ballad *Mother's Last Words*, 'a story of two boys kept from evil courses by their mother's last words', which sold over a million copies. Mary Sewell even 'wrote' *Black Beauty* in the most literal sense – Anna dictated the novel to her, or wrote portions of the book on scraps of paper, which her mother then transcribed. The writing of *Black Beauty* was a team effort.

The Dunwich Horror

If you had to nominate the town or city in England that had suffered the worst decline – I mean decline almost to the point of total extinction – you could do worse than propose the town of Dunwich in Suffolk.

Dunwich was once a major town: at its height, it boasted eight churches and was the second biggest port in medieval England after London. The town is mentioned in a twelfth-century poem by the wonderfully named Jordan Fantosme, who described the siege of Dunwich in 1173, when the townspeople successfully defended themselves against the Earl of Leicester, who was forced to retreat.

What happened to turn Dunwich from England's second biggest port to nothing more than a small East Anglian coastal village? It all began on New Year's Day 1286 when a violent storm tore along the coast of East Anglia, both Norfolk and neighbouring Suffolk, causing extensive damage to much of the town. As if that wasn't bad enough, the following year another storm hit. In 1347, powerful gales carried away 400 houses from the town. A year later, when the Black Death arrived in England, the people of Dunwich must have begun to think they were being specifically targeted for some collective sin. The final straw came in January 1362, when a fierce Atlantic gale wiped out what remained of the town. As the travel writer Annie Berlyn put it in *Sunrise-land: Rambles in Eastern England* (1894), it had become 'Dunwich the desolate, the city of the dead' and 'a heap of ruins, a handful of crumbling grey stones'. And that was the end of Dunwich.

Or not quite. The town would never again be the great port town that it had once been, but it wouldn't quite disappear into the mists of history altogether. In the early seventeenth century, it was still significant enough to attract Shakespeare's company, the King's Men, to play there in 1605–6, and again in 1608–9 and 1610–11. Sadly, there is no record of what they performed during their visit, but one assumes it wasn't *The Tempest*.

In the Victorian era, too, writers came to Dunwich in their droves. Edward FitzGerald visited while translating his popular *Rubáiyát of Omar Khayyám* in the 1850s. The humourist Jerome K. Jerome, best known for *Three Men in a Boat*, spent a number of holidays there. Algernon Charles Swinburne and Henry James also visited, as did Edward Thomas in the early twentieth century, staying in a cottage a short distance from All Saints' church, which was precariously balanced on the eroded cliff. He wrote in 1908, 'Oh Dunwich is beautiful. I am on a heaving moor of heather and close gorse up and down and ending in a sandy cliff about 80 feet perpendicular and the black, peat-strewn fine sand below. On the edge of this 1½ miles away is the ruined church that has half fallen over already. Four arches and a broken tower, pale and airy.' Eleven years later, the tower of the church succumbed to the waves.

The Wise Man of Manningtree

Manningtree in Essex has one reasonably well-known claim to fame, and 'claim' is entirely the right word: it's possibly the smallest town in the UK, with just 911 inhabitants recorded in the 2011 census. But it also bears a memorial stone to one of the unsung heroes of English literature – or, specifically, to that unsung and largely anonymous 'genre' of literature, the humble proverb.

Thomas Tusser (*circa* 1524–80) was born in Essex but became a farmer in the small village of Cattawade in neighbouring Suffolk in the 1550s. Even as a farmer, he was a significant and influential force, introducing the cultivation of barley to the region. He would live and work in East Anglia for the rest of his life, mostly as a farmer.

In 1557, the first version of Tusser's greatest work, *Hundredth Good Pointes of Husbandrie* (1557), a monthly guide to practical rural life written in rough rhyming verse, was published. It was the product of a number of years, with its wisdom derived from Tusser's experience of farming the land in Suffolk, but its wisdom went beyond the wheatfield. Indeed, Tusser's book is arguably, after the biblical Book of Proverbs, the most influential proverb-book ever written. *Hundredth Good Pointes* gave us many well-known proverbs, many of which are still in use today, albeit with slightly different wording: 'sweet April showers doth bring forth May flowers', 'at Christmas play and make good cheer, for Christmas comes but once a year', 'naught venture, naught have', 'a woman's work is never done', 'sow dry and set wet', 'bear and forbear', 'safe bind, safe find', 'who goeth a borrowing, goeth a sorrowing', 'there's no place like home', 'seek home for rest for home is best', and 'a fool and his money are soon parted'. (Tusser also provides the first known use of the word 'coxcomb', referring to a jester's cap and also, by extension, a fool.) If he'd been born four centuries later, one suspects Tusser would have been a brilliant advertising copywriter.

Hundredth Good Pointes went through numerous editions and it's been suggested that it was the bestselling book of poetry in the reign of Elizabeth I. Country wisdom is clearly what people were after. Not that the book's popularity did much for Tusser's bank balance; he died in 1580 in London and was buried in the churchyard of the gloriously named St Mildred Poultry. As Thomas Fuller colourfully described him, in a phrase that has the ring of a good Tusserian proverb, Tusser 'spread his bread with all sorts of butter; yet none could stick thereon'. The fate of the proverbialist is to recede into anonymity. Yet the willing pilgrim can find, in Manningtree church, a tablet commemorating England's greatest proverb-maker.

Letters from Mayfair

Tusser died in London, which is where we now arrive to celebrate another unsung literary hero.

He was the first African to vote in British elections, and the first to be given an obituary in the British press when he died in 1780. He was friends with both Laurence Sterne and David Garrick. A talented musician, he published his own compositions and wrote *A Theory of Music*. Thomas Gainsborough painted his portrait. Thomas Jefferson admired his writing. The posthumous publication of his letters revealed a man of warmth, humour, and humanity – qualities which many eighteenth-century readers were shocked to find in an African writer. In these and a myriad other ways, he was a pioneer. Yet these days the name Ignatius Sancho means little or nothing to most people. Who was he?

Born on an Atlantic slave ship heading for the West Indies in the late 1720s, he became an orphan at a young age, his mother dying shortly after their arrival in New Grenada and his father committing suicide as a preferable alternative to a life of slavery. Young Ignatius's owner sent him to Greenwich, where he was given to three women who gave him the surname 'Sancho' on account of his supposed resemblance to Sancho Panza, Don Quixote's squire. Sancho's new owners didn't intend to look after him especially well – they believed that keeping him ignorant would make him more obedient – but fortunately,

Sancho was to have a chance encounter that would change his life.

One day, the Duke of Montagu, who lived nearby, met young Sancho and was sufficiently impressed by the boy's promise to take him under his wing, providing him with books and championing his education at every possible opportunity. When the duke died, his widow took Sancho on as her butler, and then, when she died, he became a valet to the new duke. A few years before his death, with the duke's financial help, he opened a grocery shop at 20 Charles Street in Mayfair (the address where the future prime minister, the Earl of Rosebery, would later be born). He owned the shop outright, and his status as a male householder made him eligible to vote in elections – making him the first African to do so in Britain.

Ignatius Sancho struck up a friendly correspondence with Laurence Sterne after he wrote to him in 1766 to thank the *Tristram Shandy* author for highlighting the plight of slaves. 'I am sure you will applaud me for beseeching you to give one half hour's attention to slavery as it is this day practised in our West Indies,' he wrote. 'That subject, handled in your striking manner, would ease the yoke (perhaps) of many,' he continued, in the hope that Sterne would continue to use his high profile and popularity to bring to light the misery of slavery.

It probably won't surprise many people to learn that, alongside all this recognition, Sancho also encountered quite a lot of racial prejudice. A man in the street once shouted at him, 'Smoke Othello!' to which Sancho replied, in a thundering voice, 'Aye, sir, such Othellos you meet with but once in a century. Such Iagos as you, we meet with in every dirty passage. Proceed, sir!' Which has to be one of the greatest – not to mention one of the most eighteenth-century – retorts ever made to a racist insult.

Shortly after his death, his letters to Sterne and many others were published to over 1,200 subscribers as *The Letters of the Late Ignatius Sancho, an African*. These are of both historical and literary importance: historical because of the contemporary events which Sancho witnessed (including the Gordon 'No Popery' riots of 1780, shortly before he died), and literary because they are among the earliest writings by an African author living in Britain.

The Lion of Fleet Street

The eighteenth century was a great time to be a writer like Ignatius Sancho, if you had the right opportunities. It was at this time that Fleet Street became home to the British newspaper industry, after the *Daily Courant* was established from a house overlooking the sewage-ridden River Fleet in 1702.

Dr Johnson worked on his *Dictionary* in Gough Square, not far from Fleet Street; his house is now a museum. A statue of his cat, Hodge, can be found in the street. Johnson cut his teeth as a journalist for the Fleet Street newspapers and periodicals, but alongside the explosion in the newspaper industry, Fleet Street was also the home of another relatively recent institution: the coffee house, where people would go to read the news and discuss it. Indeed, Fleet Street could boast the very first Nando's in London – Nando's Coffee House, that is, which was up and running by 1696 and could be found next door to the shop of the bookseller Bernard Lintot. The poet and early landscape gardener William Shenstone (1714–63) wrote to his friend Richard Jago in March 1744: 'I lodge between the two coffee-houses, George's and Nando's, so that I partake of the expensiveness of both.' (Talking of expensiveness, three years earlier Shenstone had become the first known person to record the famous long word 'floccinaucinihilipilification', a jocular term supposedly coined by schoolboys at Eton, and meaning the action or habit of estimating something as worthless.)

Coffee houses were a big part of Londoners' social lives

in the eighteenth century. Jonathan Swift observed, 'It is the folly of too many, to mistake the echo of a London coffee-house for the voice of the kingdom', yet you'd have been hard-pushed to find a better way of gauging the popular mood or quickly becoming clued up on the latest news. Coffee houses could even be sources of literary creation: Button's coffee house on Russell Street near Covent Garden (now, fittingly enough, the site of a Starbucks) even boasted a white marble lion's head nailed to the wall, with customers being invited to feed letters and poems into the animal's mouth. The best submissions were published (in a feature named 'Roarings of the Lion') in the *Guardian* – not the modern-day one, but a short-lived London newspaper published in 1712–13 and founded by Richard Steele. For obvious reasons, this quick-fire, not to mention two-way, method of public communication has been likened to modern-day social media.

Fleet Street wasn't just about newspapers and coffee houses; it was also known for its 'freak shows'. These included 'Mrs Salmon's waxworks', established in 1711 (some fifty years before the more famous Madame Tussaud was even born), which featured among its exhibits (if that is quite the word) a woman who gave birth to 365 children at once and a life-size model of the prophetess Mother Shipton, which gave the unsuspecting visitor a kick on their way out. And Fleet Street would take on a new macabre tinge in the 1840s, when the popular Sweeney Todd serials established his (entirely fictional) barbershop there.

The River Fleet didn't just give its name to the famous street; it also became the name of a notorious prison – after Newgate, perhaps the most infamous of London's prisons during the period. And it is to Newgate that we now travel.

The Poet of Newgate

Newgate Prison was notorious for its unsanitary conditions. For over seven centuries, it was a lice-ridden, overcrowded den of starvation and disease. Prisoners who could afford to purchase alcohol, it was said, passed their time in perpetual drunkenness. Nevertheless, it was in such unpropitious surroundings that the tradition of women's poetry in English was effectively born, at least if one believes a man named John Bale. For Newgate Gaol was also the place where a young woman named Anne Askew, one of the first female poets to compose in the English language, is thought to have 'written' a ballad while she was imprisoned there in the 1540s.

Askew (sometimes spelt Ayscough or Ascue) was born in around 1521, the daughter of William Askew, a Lincolnshire sheriff and MP who was one of the jurors at the trial of Anne Boleyn's co-accused. He forced his daughter to marry a man named Thomas Kyme, who had been due to marry Anne's older sister, Martha, until Martha died before the marriage could take place. The problem was, Thomas Kyme was a Catholic and Anne was a Protestant reformer and so she didn't exactly go willingly into the marriage. But she had to comply with her father's wishes, and bore Kyme two children – before he eventually threw her out of the house for being Protestant. Askew responded by demanding a divorce on scriptural grounds, making her probably the first Englishwoman to make such a request. Robert Persons would later write sniffily that Anne sought a divorce in order 'to gad up and downe the countrey a ghospelling and ghossipinge where she might and ought not'. But as Persons was a Jesuit priest and not especially sympathetic (to put it mildly) to Protestants like Anne, we should perhaps take his references to Anne's 'ghossipinge' with a pinch of salt.

Indeed, this was a dangerous time to be a Protestant in England. Askew was born just a few years after Martin Luther had nailed his Ninety-five Theses to the church door at Wittenberg, signalling the start of the Protestant Reformation, and although by the 1540s the Reformation under Thomas Cromwell had led to many dramatic changes in the English Church – the most notable being the placing of English Bibles on church pulpits and the declaring of King Henry VIII as head of the Church of England – being too outspoken a reformer could still land you in trouble, in jail, or worse still, at the stake.

Such a fate awaited Anne, though by the time she was dragged to the stake she had already notched up another notable 'first', though not a particularly pleasant one: in 1546, she became the only woman to be burnt at the stake having also been tortured in the Tower of London. Torturers were often reluctant to rack a woman, which entailed stretching the victim on a wooden frame until their joints were dislocated and the pain became un-bearable, though it is believed that Askew was subjected to that ordeal shortly before she was publicly burnt. Clearly her 'ghospelling' had got up the noses of the authorities.

But Anne's legacy was not merely religious but literary: she is now chiefly remembered for 'The Ballad Which

Anne Askew Made and Sang When She Was in Newgate',
which begins:

> Like as the armed knight
> Appointed to the field,
> With this world will I fight
> And Faith shall be my shield.
>
> Faith is that weapon strong
> Which will not fail at need.
> My foes, therefore, among
> Therewith will I proceed.
>
> As it is had in strength
> And force of Christes way
> It will prevail at length
> Though all the devils say nay.

At least, she *may* have composed this ballad: some
scholars have doubted the attribution. It first appeared in
The lattre examinacyon of Anne Askewe, a book published a
year after her death, but John Bale, the editor of the work,
may well have been putting words in Askew's mouth.
(Bale's other claim to fame is that he wrote the oldest
surviving verse-drama, *Kynge Johan*, over half a century
before Shakespeare wrote *King John*.) After such a long
time, we cannot be sure, but 'The Ballad Which Anne
Askew Made and Sang When She Was in Newgate'
provides a valuable window on a bloody and momentous
era in English history.

A Coward at Hatchards

London is home to many bookshops, but Hatchards is perhaps the most distinguished of the lot. Opened in 1797 at 173 Piccadilly, but later moved to its present site at 187 Piccadilly, it is the oldest bookshop in Britain that is still trading. John Hatchard, the founder of the shop, was also a publisher: the first thing he published was a pamphlet *Reform or Run* (1797) by John Bowdler, the brother of the more famous Thomas Bowdler, who, along with their sister Harriet, attained notoriety for 'bowdlerising' Shakespeare.

Hatchards has been the bookshop of choice for many illustrious figures over the centuries. Notable customers and clients have included Queen Charlotte (the wife of George III), the Duke of Wellington, Lord Byron, William Gladstone, Benjamin Disraeli, Oscar Wilde, and Rudyard Kipling. The Royal Horticultural Society – then a small group of just seven men – held its inaugural meeting at Hatchards in 1804.

While the First World War was raging, a teenage Noël Coward stole his books from Hatchards: on one occasion, the future playwright and songwriter walked in and began stuffing books into a suitcase which, it turns out, he'd stolen from Fortnum & Mason next door. He later returned to help himself to more titles. When a shop assistant confronted him, he replied, 'Really, look how badly this shop is run! I could have made off with a dozen books and no one would have noticed.' He then walked out. The young Coward had already honed his light-fingered skills at other London stores: he stole his socks from Savile Row, and his comics from W. H. Smith.

Hatchards is thankfully still standing, which is more than can be said for Paternoster Row, the street that once stood next to St Paul's Cathedral and was described as 'almost synonymous' with literature and publishing in Britain. That is, until the events of one night, 29–30 December 1940, destroyed it forever in the course of a particularly heavy air raid during the Blitz. The event was later described as the Second Great Fire of London. As Eloise Millar and Sam Jordison record in their hugely readable account of the city, *Literary London*, some 5 million books, including the stock of around twenty publishing houses, are thought to have been destroyed in the fire. The street was rebuilt as Paternoster Square, an urban development where stock-brokers rather than publishers now ply their trade (the area is the centre of the London Stock Exchange).

A Corner of Westminster Abbey

The Irish novelist Amanda McKittrick Ros – the notoriously bad writer who so amused the Inklings in Oxford – also, you'll be delighted to hear, wrote poetry. Her poem 'Visiting Westminster Abbey' opens:

> Holy Moses! Take a look!
> Flesh decayed in every nook!
> Some rare bits of brain lie here,
> Mortal loads of beef and beer.

If that doesn't make you want to throw your rucksack over your shoulder and head to the Abbey for a day out, then frankly I'm not sure what it'll take to get you there.

Westminster Abbey was so named to contrast it with the 'minster' in the east of London, St Paul's Cathedral. The Abbey is home to probably the most famous collection of memorials and graves of poets in the world: Poets' Corner. Although Geoffrey Chaucer was the first to be buried in Poets' Corner, his interment in that part of the Abbey only took place in 1556, over a century and a half after his death. He had originally been buried elsewhere in the building, following his death in 1400, and he earned his place in the Abbey in the first place not for his poetry but for his other career: he was Clerk of Works for the Palace of Westminster. Poets' Corner would only come into being many years after Chaucer's death.

This accounts for the fact that not everyone buried in Poets' Corner was a poet, or a writer of any stripe. In amongst the poets and playwrights, you'll find the tomb of an architect (Robert Adam), a mathematician (Isaac Barrow), and even a headmaster (Richard Busby, who was head of Westminster School during the seventeenth century). George Frederic Handel is also buried in Poets' Corner, as are Henry Irving (the first actor to be knighted) and Laurence Olivier. Thomas Parr, known as 'Old Parr', got himself buried there in 1635 purely because he had, so it is claimed, lived to the extraordinary age of 152. The dancer Eva Marie Veigel (1724–1822) is also interred here.

Conversely, some high-profile writers, such as Aphra Behn, Charles Kingsley, and Sir Edward Bulwer-Lytton, are buried in Westminster Abbey but not in Poets' Corner itself. Even Shakespeare's great contemporary Ben Jonson is not in Poets' Corner, but nearby. He was buried standing up to save on the cost of the monument. His tomb misspells his name as 'Johnson'.

Browning in Berkeley Square

There may be no record of a nightingale singing in Berkeley Square, but there's a recording of Robert Browning doing so – or, at any rate, reciting his poetry. On 7 April 1889 at his home at 15 Berkeley Square, Rudolf Lehmann held a dinner party at which Browning (another celebrated inhabitant of Poets' Corner) became the first poet to have his voice recorded on a phonograph.

Browning had been born in London in 1812. At age fourteen, he wrote a poem, 'The Dance of Death', in which Ague, Consumption, Fever, Madness, and Pestilence compete for the title of man's worst foe; this early poem features many of the macabre hallmarks of his later poetry, dealing with death, murder, and ugliness (physical and moral) as it so often does. Although he studied at the University of London, he was as much self-taught as formally educated; he dropped out of his studies after just one year. His early work included a long narrative poem called *Sordello* (1840), which to most Victorian readers proved impenetrable. Thomas Carlyle's wife Jane read the entire thing – nearly 6,000 lines – without ever working out whether Sordello was a man, a city, or a book. 'Obscurity' is often a charge, or sometimes a compliment, laid at Robert Browning's door.

Fittingly, *Sordello* is about a poet who never quite makes it in the world, and Browning's own rise to literary recognition and financial success was a slow and unsteady one.

Elizabeth Barrett, who became his wife in 1846, was the far more successful of the two during her lifetime. But by the time he attended Lehmann's dinner party in April 1889, the aged Browning was finally established as one of the great poets of the age – after Tennyson, perhaps the most famous. And although the recording of Tennyson reading his poem 'The Charge of the Light Brigade' was one of the earliest instances of a poet allowing his voice to be committed to shellac, Tennyson wasn't the very first.

At the dinner party, Rudolf Lehmann had a Thomas Edison phonograph with him, and persuaded Browning to say something into it. The poet dutifully obliged, and began to recite his poem 'How They Brought the Good News from Ghent to Aix':

I sprang to the saddle, and Joris, and he;
I galloped, Dirck galloped, we galloped all three;
'Speed!' echoed the wall to us galloping through;
'Speed!' echoed the – er – [pause]
Then the gates shut behind us, the lights sank to rest [pause]

Which is rather different from the version you'll find printed in Browning's *Collected Poems*, because he'd forgotten the words to his own poem.

In fairness, Browning was an old man of seventy-six when he made this recording; before the year was out, he would be dead. However, memory lapses appear to have been a lifelong problem. When asked to respond to a toast at a Royal Literary Fund dinner in 1846, Browning managed to ramble on for several minutes without once mentioning his intended subject.

Building Brick Lane

Brick Lane offers a nice insight into the changing face
of London through the centuries. Once upon a time, it
was a Roman burial ground. Then it became known as
Whitechapel Lane. In the fifteenth century, when bricks
and tiles began to be manufactured there, it acquired its
current name. In the seventeenth century, its famous market
was established, around the same time as French Huguenots
started to settle in the area, and this part of London became
known more for weaving and cloth-making than for bricks.

Brick Lane has been the home of immigrant communities,
then, for a long time. In the nineteenth century, Irish people
fleeing the Great Famine settled in the street, as did
Ashkenazi Jews escaping persecution in eastern Europe.
Then, during the last few decades of the twentieth century,
immigrants from Bangladesh began to make their homes in
the area. The Bangladeshi community in this part of Tower
Hamlets was brought to wider attention when Monica Ali's
debut novel *Brick Lane* was published in 2003. But as Sukhdev
Sandhu pointed out when reviewing Ali's novel for the
London Review of Books, Bengali immigrants had been settling
in this part of London for some 200 years, ever since lascars
– soldiers from Asia serving in the British Navy – had
arrived, 'ragged and penniless' in Sandhu's phrase, in
London's docks and decided to drop anchor there for good.

Ali was named one of Granta's Best of Young British
Novelists before she had published a single word of her

debut novel. When *Brick Lane* appeared, it garnered praise from scores of reviewers and many more readers. Taking the titular London road as its focus – and Brick Lane has been, since the 1970s, synonymous with the Bangladeshi community – Ali's novel was almost Dickensian in its ability to be very, very funny while also tackling hard-hitting subject matter: the novel treats a number of unsettling themes including rape, suicide, and disfigurement (one of the women in the novel has acid thrown in her face), while one of the characters turns to prostitution as an alternative to starving on the streets.

Brick Lane focuses on Nazneen, a young woman brought up in Bangladesh who enters into an arranged marriage with Chanu, a man nearly twice her age, with whom she moves to London. Balanced against this is the story of Nazneen's sister Hasina, who effectively did the opposite and fled Bangladesh to elope with the man she loved, becoming an outcast from the family as a result (although Nazneen keeps in touch with her). Nazneen and Chanu's marriage is fraught with problems, and she is eventually drawn into the arms of another man, Karim, whom she meets while she is taking on some sewing work (in a nod back to Brick Lane's strong tailoring tradition) to provide additional income for her and her husband.

In 2006, when *Brick Lane* was being adapted for the big screen, there were reports of members of London's Bangladeshi community protesting over the film because of the way Ali's novel depicted British Bangladeshis (especially Chanu, who is one of the novel's chief sources of humour), although Ali herself observed that media coverage had blown such 'protests' out of proportion. Indeed, hundreds of locals turned up to auditions for the film, hoping to be cast as extras.

Dawn at Billingsgate

We linger in London for a while longer, coming to Billingsgate fish market at four in the morning. Why? To pay homage to the starting point of a curious Victorian book offering a detailed picture of life in London.

In 1925, Virginia Woolf published her modernist novel *Mrs Dalloway*, a book set over the course of a single day in mid June 1923 (the specific date she had in mind, it has been speculated, was Wednesday 13 June). The novel is about, as Woolf herself proclaims, 'life; London; this moment of June'. Other authors who have written a novel set on just one day in London are Ian McEwan and John Lanchester, who may well have had Woolf's earlier novel in mind. Woolf herself clearly owed a debt to James Joyce's *Ulysses*, which had been published in 1922 and is set on one day in Dublin, 16 June 1904.

But modernists like Woolf and Joyce didn't invent the concept of writing a book covering the events of just one day in a major city. The writer who should get the credit for that innovation was, in fact, not a novelist at all, although he had novelistic aspirations. His name was George Augustus Sala (1828–95), and he was one of the most intriguing men to grace British journalism during the entire nineteenth century.

Sala was born in Dorset Square in Marylebone, London, the product of a fling between a Guyanese actress and an army captain. His long journalistic career began in 1851 when he submitted an article, 'The Key of the Street', to Dickens's periodical *Household Words*. William Makepeace Thackeray thought it 'almost the best magazine paper that ever was written', and Sala soon became established as one of the leading reporters of the age, and was one of the first star writers for the *Daily Telegraph* when it was launched in 1855.

Sala came up with the idea of writing an account – semi-fictionalised, although relying heavily on his first-hand observations of real life – of a typical day in contemporary London. He called the resulting book *Twice Round the Clock* (incidentally, the year his account was published, 1859, was also the year that Big Ben first rang out – a bell whose chimes resonate through Woolf's later circadian book, *Mrs Dalloway*), and the book charts a day in the life of the city, beginning at Billingsgate fish market at dawn. Sala himself was modest about his project, claiming that 'the idea of thus chronicling, hour by hour, the shifting panorama of London life was not original', and indeed the idea of reporting on the 'Hours of London' can be traced back to a *Spectator* essay of 1712 written by Richard Steele. But Sala's book offered an important new take on this idea, recording the impressions of life in the bustling metropolis during the Victorian era, with a Dickensian eye for detail.

Sala also wrote pornography, contributing to the 1882 novel *The Mysteries of Verbena House*, a tale of saucy goings-on at an all-girls' school described by noted collector of erotica, Henry Spencer Ashbee, as 'one of the best books of its kind', though that's not much of an endorsement of its literary merits. Sala wasn't always an entirely pleasant man: he once successfully sued a fellow journalist, James Hain Friswell, for libellously suggesting he had once been imprisoned for debt, even though he had been. He earned a good deal of money from his journalism, but was even better at spending it. Now his name is little known, but *Twice Round the Clock* is a valuable record of everyday life in Victorian London and inadvertently pre-empted modern fiction's later preoccupation with one-day novels.

A Book on Trial at Bow Street

On 9 November 1928 at Bow Street Magistrate's Court, a book went on trial. Several months earlier, D. H. Lawrence had published his novel *Lady Chatterley's Lover* in Italy, but it would not be until 1960 that that book would be the centre of a much-publicised court case. In 1928, however, another novel found itself in the dock. It was called *The Well of Loneliness*, and the charge, as with *Chatterley* several decades later, was one of obscenity.

The Well of Loneliness, by Radclyffe Hall, focuses on Stephen Gordon, an Englishwoman (christened with the male name her disappointed parents, expecting a baby boy, went ahead and gave their daughter anyway) who discovers that she is an 'invert', to use Hall's own word, at a young age. Like Radclyffe Hall herself, Stephen feels herself to be a man trapped in a woman's body, and she ends up getting involved with two women, sharing 'schoolgirlish kisses' with her neighbour's American wife and later falling in love with Mary, whom she meets while driving ambulances in the First World War.

Shortly after it arrived on the shelves, a campaign arose to get the novel banned. The man leading the charge was James Douglas, editor of the *Sunday Express*, who declared, in words that left his views on the novel in little doubt, 'I would rather give a healthy boy or a healthy girl a phial of prussic acid than this novel.' In an editorial of August 1928, he likened lesbians to lepers and cast himself as the guardian of the nation's morals, defending Britain against the 'moral danger' of same-sex relationships as depicted in Hall's novel. The impact was swift and destructive.

As Diana Souhami observes in *The Trials of Radclyffe Hall*, on the day of the trial a number of high-profile witnesses, including Virginia Woolf and E. M. Forster, A. E. Housman's brother Laurence, the biologist Julian Huxley, and Rabbi Joseph Frederick Stern, all turned out to take to the stand and defend the novel against the obscenity charge. (Woolf was a reluctant witness: she declared that she couldn't be entirely sure the novel wasn't indecent, because she found it so dull that she was unable to keep her eyes on the page.) Norman Haire, an Australian sexologist, expressed the then remarkably enlightened medical opinion that homosexuality was genetic and a reader could no more be made homosexual by reading this novel than one could become syphilitic by reading about syphilis.

But this was all in vain. Even the notion of defending the book's literary merit – which was what helped to acquit *Lady Chatterley's Lover* at the later and far more famous trial – had been rendered futile by Douglas's declaration that a well-written obscene book was more dangerous than a badly written obscene one. A week later, the judge passed his verdict – namely, that the book be immediately banned, with all copies then in existence to be destroyed.

In some ways, Radclyffe Hall was unlucky. Other writers had treated the subject of female same-sex desire in fiction and got away with it. Indeed, another novel containing lesbianism, Virginia Woolf's *Orlando*, came out (as it were) the same year, but it was neither banned nor put on trial, despite being based loosely on Woolf's real-life friend and lover, Vita Sackville-West. What made the banning of *The Well of Loneliness* even more remarkable was that there was no sexual content in it at all, beyond the statement 'she kissed her full on the lips like a lover' and the suggestive, but hardly pornographic, line 'and that night, they were not divided'. I've read racier tax returns. The rest, it would seem, existed in readers' imaginations.

Almost exactly thirty-two years later, on 10 November 1960, *Lady Chatterley's Lover* would go on sale in Britain having been cleared of charges of obscenity. It would become a bestseller. By this time, *The Well of Loneliness* was back in print – it had been, without risk of prosecution, since 1949 – and was selling an estimated 100,000 copies in the US every year. (Hall herself didn't live to see this, having died in 1943.) Although it had been the subject of two trials in the States, her novel had been cleared in both cases. In 1974, the novel's status as an 'acceptable' novel was confirmed by the BBC, when it was serialised on the radio as a *Book at Bedtime*.

Shere Folly

We'll move out to leafy Surrey for the next leg of our literary journey. On a summer's day in 1887, J. M. Barrie, best known for creating Peter Pan, was in the Surrey village of Shere and came up with an idea. He and a group of friends would form their own cricket team and challenge the local side to a match. It wasn't perhaps the worst idea he'd ever come up with, but it wasn't far off.

Barrie had a fondness for games of all kinds – he even invented several of his own, which bear the intriguing names 'egg-cap' and 'capey-dykey' – but cricket was his chief passion. As Kevin Telfer reveals in *Peter Pan's First XI: The Story of J. M. Barrie's Cricket Team*, Barrie's fondness for cricket inspired him to set about forming the Allahakbarries – effectively the first celebrity cricket team – which over the next few decades would boast some of the most celebrated writers of the day: H. G. Wells, Sir Arthur Conan Doyle (who would later support the campaign to ban *The Well of Loneliness* and other indecent literature), G. K. Chesterton, Jerome K. Jerome, P. G. Wodehouse, and A. A. Milne. (Milne and Wells already knew each other: a young Wells had taught an even younger Milne at school.) Tennyson's son was also on the team, as was the creator of the amateur cracksman, Raffles – and son-in-law of Doyle – E. W. Hornung. The name Allahakbarries was down to an error in translation. A couple of team members laboured under the mistaken belief that the Arabic phrase *Allah akbar* meant 'heaven help us' rather than 'God is great'. But the name stuck, not least because of the pleasing fact that it contained Barrie's name.

In any case, 'heaven help us' would have worked well as the team's slogan. The Allahakbarries may have boasted some of the finest and most successful writers of the age, but they weren't exactly promising cricketing material. During the train journey on their way to their first match, Barrie realised that one of his players didn't even know which side of the bat to hit the ball with. Another player had turned up to the railway station in his pyjamas. Barrie said of his own bowling technique: 'After delivering the ball I would sit at mid-on to wait until it reached the other end, which it sometimes did.' The result of their first match at Shere was really never in doubt.

But exactly how badly did Barrie's team of largely incompetent cricketers fare at that first match? Unfortunately, we don't know – their score-keeping was about as efficient as their play – but it looks as though they had a very short innings, and decided to call it a day when the local innkeeper playing on the opposing team stepped out to bat again. At that point, the Allahakbarries all expressed a sudden desire to repair to the batsman's inn, the White Horse, to dine. The pub is still open for business. In 1890, Barrie wrote a short book about his team of celebrity cricketers, *Allahakbarries CC*, which was privately printed and remains difficult to find, at least for a reasonable price, but which contains more insights into their cricketing adventures.

The Allahakbarries may have been sporting amateurs, but there was one exception: Sir Arthur Conan Doyle.

The creator of Sherlock Holmes actually played first-class matches for the Marylebone Cricket Club and even managed to bowl out none other than the celebrated batsman W. G. Grace during one match. If the rest of the team had been so gifted, the Allahakbarries might have become more than a knockabout group of sporting dilettantes – but then where would be the fun in that?

Anyone for Tennis at Witley

Surrey isn't just renowned (if that's quite the word) for its links with literary cricketers. It's also the place where modern tennis was born.

Well, sort of. The first reference to modern tennis in the *Oxford English Dictionary* – that is, lawn tennis as opposed to real tennis, which had been around for centuries – is in a letter written by George Eliot in August 1878. This was one year after the first Wimbledon championship was held, so we can assume that others had got there before the author of *Middlemarch*, but the *OED* cites Eliot's letter as the first recorded use of the word in reference to the modern game.

In the small village of Witley, a few miles south-west of Godalming, Eliot bought The Heights in 1877. She lived there with her common-law husband G. H. Lewes. Eliot and Lewes had been in a relationship for over twenty years: even though Lewes was already married when they met, he and his wife had an open marriage (as well as the three children she had with Lewes, she had also borne four children with the son of the poet Leigh Hunt), and Lewes was unable to get a divorce. But although their domestic set-up was unconventional by Victorian standards, Eliot and Lewes became, along with the Brownings, the most famous literary couple of the Victorian age. Although Eliot wrote most frequently about the Midlands where she had grown up, she wrote all of her novels while living in

London and Surrey, using the memories of her childhood and youth spent in Warwickshire as inspiration for her fiction.

It was at The Heights that a young man named John Walter Cross introduced Eliot – whose real name was Mary Ann Evans – to tennis in 1877. Cross was an admirer of Eliot's work who had been introduced to her and Lewes by their friend, and Eliot's onetime romantic interest, Herbert Spencer, the man who coined the phrase 'survival of the fittest' to describe Darwinian evolution.

Unfortunately, the last couple of years of Eliot's life were to be marred by tragedy and misfortune. In 1878, the same year that Eliot made that inaugural reference to lawn tennis, Lewes suddenly fell ill and died. Eliot became a recluse for several months afterwards, but in May 1880 she agreed to marry John Cross, her friend and tennis coach. But even on their honeymoon Cross began to display worryingly odd behaviour. In Venice, he jumped out of their hotel room into the Grand Canal, and appeared to suffer some sort of breakdown, losing a considerable amount of weight. After their return to England, however, they passed a happy summer and autumn at The Heights, but by the end of the year Eliot was dead, having fallen ill with kidney disease.

Eliot's gravestone in Highgate Cemetery, north London, gives her pen name alongside her married name, Mary Ann Cross. The Church of England had vetoed a request for Eliot to be interred in Poets' Corner in Westminster Abbey, because of her previous long-term relationship with Lewes.

Gadding about the Place at Higham

George Eliot was able to buy The Heights thanks to her financial success as a novelist. In 1821, a nine-year-old Charles Dickens first clapped eyes on Gad's Hill Place, a country house in Higham, Kent, not far from Rochester. His father, who worked in the naval dockyard in nearby Chatham, showed his young son the house and told him, 'If you were to be very persevering and were to work hard, you might some day come to live in it.' Clearly Dickens junior heeded his father's words, for thirty-five years later he bought Gad's Hill Place for £1,790 from another author, Eliza Lynn Linton, whose novels and anti-feminist essays are now little read.

Gad's Hill Place is where Dickens spent much of the last fourteen years of his life, yet for much of this his wife Catherine was absent from the picture. In autumn 1857, not long after he'd bought his Kent retreat, he famously climbed out of bed at two in the morning, got dressed, and walked from his London home, Tavistock House, all the way to Gad's Hill Place – a journey of some 30 miles 'through the dead night', as he put it in a letter written shortly after. 'After all, it would be better to be up and doing something, than lying here.' Dickens often indulged in night walks, and even wrote an article with that title about his nocturnal perambulations.

Such restless behaviour was not out of the ordinary for the novelist who famously burnt himself out working – or overworking – himself into an early grave in 1870. A year after he undertook his 30-mile night-time walk, he formally separated from his wife and started a relationship with the actress Ellen Ternan, a woman twenty-seven years his junior.

One of the most glorious things in Gad's Hill Place is the fake bookcase Dickens had installed in his study, which boasts the spines of such imaginary titles as *Cat's Lives* (in nine volumes, of course), a *History of the Middling Ages*, and *Jonah's Account of the Whale*. The books had been installed first at Tavistock House in 1851, but were moved to Gad's Hill Place when he purchased his country home.

Alongside Rochester, the Kent town with the biggest claim to Dickens fame is Chatham, which until 2016 was home of the theme park, Dickens World. This included a water ride based around *Great Expectations* (which ended with passengers being dropped from a London sewer into the Thames), a 4-D film featuring an inflatable Catherine Dickens, and a soft play area called, a tad worryingly, 'Fagin's Den'. Despite the obvious lure of such attractions, Dickens World closed in 2016.

Coming to Dover

The poem that springs to mind as we continue down to Dover – which Dickens, in a letter of 1852, described as 'infinitely too genteel' and 'too bandy (I mean musical, no reference to its legs)' – is Matthew Arnold's 'Dover Beach', published in 1867 but thought to have been written in 1851, when Arnold spent the last night of his honeymoon in the town. As poems written on honeymoons go, it's pretty bleak, so one wonders what Mrs Arnold made of it. The American poet Anthony Hecht did just that, writing a riposte to Arnold's Victorian lament for the loss of religious faith, 'The Dover Bitch', which considered this honeymoon meditation from the perspective of Arnold's wife.

But Hecht isn't the only poet to respond to Arnold's poem. In 2007, a collection written by a new and then largely unknown British poet, Daljit Nagra, was published by Faber & Faber. The title of Nagra's debut volume, *Look We Have Coming to Dover!*, alluded to the title of D. H. Lawrence's third volume of poems (*Look! We Have Come Through!*), a collection by W. H. Auden (*Look, Stranger*), and, given the Dover connection, Matthew Arnold's 'Dover Beach'. Nagra's title also conjures up immigration into Britain, of course – something that Nagra, whose parents moved to Britain from India in the 1950s before he was born, explores repeatedly in his work. (The title poem in his debut volume contains the word 'cushy', an Urdu word which was introduced into English by Rudyard

Kipling, another key writer whose work Nagra engages with.)

As Rachel Cooke commented when reviewing Nagra's debut in the *Guardian* in 2007, *Look We Have Coming to Dover!* references everything from arranged marriages and corner shops to KFC and Hilda Ogden from *Coronation Street*. Critics and authors disagree over how useful a term like 'British-Asian' really is – the hyphen implying a bridge but also a gap, a sign of doubleness and difference – but Nagra's poetry shows how contemporary Britain, especially for Nagra, is a fusion of different traditions and different nationalities.

Perhaps the deftest way he does this is through allusions to previous British writers, many of whom themselves incorporated multiple nationalities: Rudyard Kipling (British, but born in imperial India), W. H. Auden (born in Yorkshire, but later to move to the States and earn a different hyphenation, 'Anglo-American'), and Ford Madox Ford (English, but half German – one of Nagra's poems, 'Parade's End', shares its title with Ford's sequence of novels about the First World War). Nagra himself got bitten by the poetry bug after he bought a volume of William Blake's poems and decided he wanted to study English literature; he later became a teacher of English in a London school.

As a poet closely associated with Nagra's publisher, Faber & Faber – namely, T. S. Eliot – once observed, the poet should use tradition in order to underscore what makes his own work new and distinctive. A contemporary poet writes as if he is channelling the poetic tradition through his words, but in doing so, highlights how he is adding to that tradition. Part of Nagra's skill is the way he draws on the canon of English poetry in order to show how the experiences of a contemporary British Asian writer both extend and invite us to question important aspects of the past: the British Empire, for one (back to Kipling again).

Nagra's poetry is also in a long line of British poetry that celebrates the comic as well as the serious, and he realises how closely they have fed off each other in English literature ever since Geoffrey Chaucer. Of his debut volume, Nagra himself said it contained 'silly stories' as well as gossip and 'slapstick'. But his poetry does carry serious intent: as he pointed out, there hasn't been much popular poetry written about the Indian working classes in Britain. Being published by Faber & Faber, and short-listed for numerous British poetry prizes (and winning the Forward Prize for his debut), has helped Nagra to attain a level of fame that has eluded other British Indian poets.

Apples and Oranges at Etchingham

Moving along the south coast and coming inland, we find the Jacobean house, Bateman's, in Burwash, where Rudyard Kipling lived between 1902 and his death in 1936. When he first visited the house, Kipling declared 'her Spirit – her Feng Shui – to be good. We went through every room and found no shadow of ancient regrets, stifled miseries, nor any menace though the "new" end of her was three hundred years old.' In making this statement, Kipling anticipated by nearly a hundred years the British vogue for Feng Shui.

Anthony Burgess once described Kipling as 'a poet of doubt and division, with hysteria not far from the surface', which seems about right. Which is as good a reason as any to move from Bateman's along to the nearby house of Applegarth, where Burgess lived for several years.

Burgess's home in the early 1960s, Applegarth, is a semi-detached house on the High Street in the Sussex village of Etchingham, about a mile away from Kipling's home at Bateman's. According to Andrew Biswell in *The Real Life of Anthony Burgess*, Burgess spent a typical day at Applegarth smoking (up to eighty cigarettes a day), writing and reviewing (he reviewed 350 books for the *Yorkshire Post* in just over two years), and pacing around his study to offset the 'Writer's Evil', haemorrhoids. He and his wife spent the evenings watching television (again, for reviewing purposes: he wrote a television column for the *Listener* magazine) and drinking copious quantities of wine and Gordon's gin.

Even the animals of Applegarth were roped into helping around the place, like a miniature farm. One of the first things Burgess would do when he'd rolled out of bed in the morning was kick his dog, Haji, and call him a 'lazy bastard'. Meanwhile, in the back garden, a cage of guinea pigs was systematically moved around the lawn so the enslaved rodents would chew the grass and save Burgess the bother of having to mow it.

Burgess wrote about the village of Etchingham in his *Enderby* novels from this period, though he hated the villagers and didn't enjoy his time there. The Burgesses moved away in 1964 and kept the house on as a holiday home, but only for a few years. It was, however, during his time at Applegarth that Burgess embarked on a writing spree, spurred on by a cancer diagnosis that gave him only a year to live. In this period in the early 1960s, he quickly churned out a string of novels designed to provide financial support for his widow, including *The Wanting Seed* (about overpopulation) and, most famously, *A Clockwork Orange*. The diagnosis turned out to have been a misdiagnosis, and Burgess would live for another three decades.

Young at Hartfield

Kipling was also a member of the Allahakbarries, J. M. Barrie's literary cricket team, along with A. A. Milne. And if you travel about 20 miles east from Kipling's home at Burwash, you will reach Milne's home, Cotchford Farm, in Hartfield in the same county. Hartfield should be known as Poohville.

Milne bought Cotchford Farm in 1925, and it was here that he wrote *Winnie-the-Pooh* and *The House at Pooh Corner*, which introduced the Bear of Little Brain and his porcine companion to the world. As *The Oxford Guide to Literary Britain and Ireland* notes, many of the locales which turn up in Milne's Pooh books were inspired by places in and around Hartfield: Poohsticks Bridge is a real wooden bridge a couple of miles south of the village, while Gills Lap, a group of pines in Ashdown Forest, became Galleon's Lap in Milne's writing. Five Hundred Acre Wood was chopped down to size, famously, as Hundred Acre Wood. Many of the characters in Milne's fiction, too, were based on real cuddly toys owned by his son Christopher Robin Milne: the originals of Pooh, Piglet, Tigger, Eeyore, and Kanga (the prototype for Roo was sadly lost) are now housed in the New York Public Library.

The real Christopher Robin, who passed a happy childhood at Cotchford Farm, had an altogether more ambivalent attitude to his subsequent fate – like the real-life Peter Pan, he became a man who was destined to be forever linked with the fictionalised version of himself as a child. Oddly, Milne had predicted all this – even before his son was born. In 1921, four years before he moved to Hartfield, Milne had written a play, *The Great Broxopp*, in which a father, James Broxopp, uses his young son's image to sell 'beans for babies'; his son, Jack, comes to resent his father for having exploited his own son thus. The play was quickly forgotten – it closed after just eight weeks – but it seemed to foreshadow Christopher Robin's own later feelings towards his father.

In 1968, Brian Jones, the founder of the Rolling Stones, bought Cotchford Farm. A year later, he was found dead in the pool at the house, aged just twenty-seven. Milne himself had died in 1956, his *Pooh* stories having become children's classics – though sadly he didn't live to see *Winnie ille Pu*, the unlikely Latin translation of his first *Pooh* book, become the only book in Latin ever to grace the *New York Times* bestseller list in 1960.

The Train to Birmingham

Many classic children's stories have their own curious origin stories. Roger Hargreaves was inspired to write the first *Mr Men* book, *Mr Tickle*, when his son asked him what a tickle looked like. Paddington Bear came into being when Michael Bond bought a teddy bear from a shop near Paddington station, reportedly because he felt sorry for it – it was the only one left on the shelves on Christmas Eve. And the Reverend W. Awdry's railway series began life in Birmingham as short stories written to amuse his small son, who was recovering from measles.

It was while he was living and working in Birmingham – to which we now make a sudden jaunt – that Wilbert Vere Awdry (1911–97), a lifelong railway fanatic, was inspired to pen the series of stories for his son that would soon be entertaining millions of other children too. He'd only moved to Birmingham because his pacifist stance following the outbreak of the Second World War led to his being asked to leave his parish in Wiltshire. The Bishop of Birmingham offered him the job of curate at King's Norton, and it was while living here that Awdry would begin to write the stories that made him famous.

The fictional setting of the Island of Sodor, just off the English mainland near Barrow-in-Furness, came about after Awdry observed that the Isle of Man was listed as part of 'the Diocese of Sodor and Man', yet although there was an Isle of Man, there was no corresponding Island of

Sodor. It took a few books before everything began to fall into place. Thomas the Tank Engine, the most famous engine in the series, didn't actually appear in the first book. The Fat Controller was named the Fat Director until the third book, when his name was changed after the British railways were nationalised in 1948.

Then, in 1953, an early attempt to adapt the stories for television ended in disaster when, during an embarrassingly ill-prepared live broadcast, a points failure led to one of the model engines, Henry, derailing, at which point a human hand appeared in shot to get him back on track. It would be over thirty years before Awdry and his publishers let anyone from television have another go at adapting the stories. Thankfully, that later series, narrated by Ringo Starr in the 1980s, would prove a big hit with children and adults alike. The books, meanwhile, have sold an estimated 50 million copies.

A Ludlow Lad

One poet put Shropshire on the map more than any other, and he was a man who was born in Worcestershire, had his heart broken in Oxford, worked for a number of years in London, and then became a Latin professor at Cambridge, where he died. His name was A. E. Housman (1859–1936). He visited Shropshire only once, and even then it was only after most of the poems comprising his most famous volume, *A Shropshire Lad*, had already been written in Highgate, London.

An eagle-eyed Shropshire resident will quickly suspect as much. In one poem, Housman had written: 'The vane on Hughley steeple / Veers bright, a far-known sign'. Shortly after *A Shropshire Lad* was published in 1896, the poet's brother, Laurence, visited the county and wrote back gloomily that not only did Hughley church have no steeple and no weathervane, but it was so buried within the surrounding valley that it wasn't a 'far-known sign' either. As Peter Parker points out in *Housman Country*, the poet also suggested that part of Hughley churchyard contained the graves of people who had taken their own lives, whereas in fact, Laurence reported to his brother, the graveyard was full of respectable churchwardens and vicars' wives. 'I did not apprehend that the faithful would be making pilgrimages to these holy places,' Housman later mournfully noted.

Indeed, Housman's main source of information about Shropshire was a book, *Murray's Handbook for Shropshire,*

Cheshire and Lancashire (1870), from which he took the names of many places mentioned in *A Shropshire Lad*, such as 'Clunton and Clunbury, Clungunford and Clun' – 'the quietest places under the sun', as Housman's poem, which cheerily lifts these words verbatim from *Murray's*, has it. But Housman's ability to summon up the landscape and its imagined past created some of the finest poetry about the English countryside; such as in the poem that begins 'On Wenlock Edge', which sees Housman's 'lad' musing upon an ancient Roman's view of the same landscape nearly two millennia before, when the settlement of Uriconium stood on the same spot. (Wilfred Owen would later write a poem, 'Uriconium: An Ode', about the same place.)

As a boy he had seen the distant hills of Shropshire from his home county of Worcestershire, and his poetry captured the beauty and feel of the English countryside – replete with its church bells, meadows, sheep, and young men wanting to kill themselves over a girl. In Housman's own case, it was a boy – an athlete at Oxford named Moses Jackson – who caused him lifelong heartache and inspired him to write poetry. When Jackson died in 1923, so did Housman's muse.

Housman wrote many of the sixty-three poems that make up *A Shropshire Lad* during 1895, when a 'continuous excitement' – and, by Housman's own account, a bad sore throat – helped to feed the poetry that would make him, and Shropshire, famous throughout the world. Many of us first heard of Wenlock, Ludlow, Bredon, and the marvellously named Clungunford in Housman's work. (Indeed, Bredon is actually in Housman's native Worcestershire rather than Shropshire.) Through *A Shropshire Lad*, Housman helped to create an image of rural England that has endured in the popular consciousness. Although the poems are frequently about lost or hopeless love, suicide, or depression, they also create a rousing picture of Shropshire and its markets and villages, its inns and churches. So what if the steeples aren't wholly accurate.

It may be that another event of 1895, namely the trial and subsequent imprisonment of Oscar Wilde for 'gross indecency', also had its part in bringing about Housman's miraculous flurry of poetic creativity. The Wilde trials made homosexual men like Housman far more cautious – something that Tom Stoppard brilliantly captures in *The Invention of Love*. Revealingly, in 1895, Housman wrote a poem about Wilde which he never published in *A Shropshire Lad*, and which would only see the light of day after Housman's death. Beginning 'O who is that young sinner with the handcuffs on his wrists?', the poem elliptically addresses Wilde's homosexuality by referring to another trait, 'the colour of his hair'.

A Shropshire Lad was published in 1896 at Housman's own expense, and initially it showed little sign of becoming a classic. The first print run of 500 copies took two years to sell out. But it went on to become a bestseller and was a favourite among soldiers during the First World War. For many years, Housman refused to accept any royalties for the book, considering academia his 'trade' and poetry a mere sideline.

Against the north wall of St Laurence's Church in Ludlow you can find the plaque marking the spot where Housman's ashes were interred. Inscribed on the plaque are the opening words of his 'Parta Quies' (a phrase from Virgil, meaning 'rest is won'): 'Goodnight: Ensured release, Imperishable peace: Have these for yours'.

King of Hay-on-Wye

In 1962, a man named Richard Booth bought an old fire station for £700 and opened a bookshop on Church Street in Hay-on-Wye, on the Welsh borders. At the time, Hay was a small town and things were looking bleak. A year later, as part of the Beeching cuts, the town lost its railway station. Hay didn't look like the sort of place whose economic prospects were likely to be revived any time soon.

But Booth didn't see it that way. At the time, libraries around Wales were closing, and Booth bought up their old stock and began filling his new premises with the discarded books. He bought the entire contents of a library in Ireland, discovering that many of the books had remained untouched for two centuries. Some of them were so thick with dust that handling them was, in the words of Booth himself, like 'touching the fur of a young rabbit'. Booth's idea was to accumulate old and obscure books, on the basis that somebody, somewhere would want them. He then set about quietly transforming his humble home town into the largest trading centre for second-hand books in the world. Within six years of opening, Booth's bookshop was generating an annual turnover of £100,000. With his profits, he bought the town's castle.

Booth knew how to court publicity, and on April Fools' Day 1977 he declared Hay an independent kingdom, with himself as King of Hay – King Richard, *Coeur du Livres* – and his horse, Caligula, as Prime Minister. (The town's navy, meanwhile, comprised a two-man rowing dinghy on the River Wye.) This publicity stunt helped to generate greater interest in Hay, and more visitors flocked in.

As Kate Clarke observes in *The Book of Hay*, all of this was about more than just good publicity for Booth's bookshop. His stance against big business, mass tourism, and bureaucracy, which he felt was destroying rural communities and small towns like Hay, was sincere and his declaration of Hay as a self-sufficient 'kingdom' had a serious point.

Hay's transformation into a small town with big ideas would, a decade later, be given another leg up. In 1988, a young actor and Cambridge graduate named Peter Florence and his father Norman launched a literary festival in the town, funded by the winnings of a poker game. The first festival was a modest success, featuring talks by Carol Ann Duffy and Arnold Wesker among other authors, some of whom were paid in cases of claret. Peter Florence performed a one-man show about Wilfred Owen. It took a few years for the festival to become firmly established – Arthur Miller, when invited to attend the second festival, reportedly asked if 'Hay-on-Wye' was a type of sandwich – but by 1997, visitor numbers had grown from 1,200 at the first festival to a whopping 35,000.

As a result of the enterprising spirit and ingenuity of Booth and Florence, every year around half a million people now come to a town with a population of just over 1,500. And it all started when a young man decided to shun the bright lights of London and transform the fading fortunes of his small home town. Booth later sold his original bookshop and opened another in the town – called, appropriately, the King of Hay. Whether he still has a horse, and what official role it has around the place, is not known.

Drowning in Denbighshire

It is sobering to reflect that, if it hadn't been for a jellyfish, we would never have had *Brideshead Revisited*.

This statement probably requires some qualification. Life was not looking good for Evelyn Waugh in the mid 1920s. In January 1925, not long after he'd graduated from Oxford with a third-class degree, he took a job as a school-teacher at Arnold House Preparatory School in north Wales, and quickly regretted it. He felt isolated so far away from his friends in London and Oxford. Then he received two cruel blows to his prospects. First, he got a dismissive rejection letter for his novel, a work-in-progress, and promptly burnt the manuscript. Then, shortly after, he learned that a job in Italy working as secretary to the translator Charles Scott Moncrieff, which he'd eagerly applied for, had fallen through.

According to his own account (which some biographers have questioned, but others take more or less at face value), Waugh resolved to commit suicide by drowning in the sea off the north Wales coast. After walking glumly down to the beach, he took his clothes off, left a suicide note in the form of a quotation from Euripides, and then swam out to his fate.

It was the kindly intervention of a jellyfish that saved him, after it generously decided to sting him on the shoulder just at the right moment (or the wrong one, depending on how you view it). For some reason, the sting forced Waugh to rethink his plan, and he resolved to live, swimming back to the shore where he duly tore up his suicide note, got dressed, and went home.

Waugh's experience in Denbighshire would feed directly into his first novel, *Decline and Fall* (1928). He based Captain Grimes on the master at Arnold House, while Llanddulas, the nearby village, became Llanabba Castle in the novel. He would go on to become the toast of the 1930s and 1940s, with novels such as *A Handful of Dust*, *Scoop*, and *Brideshead Revisited*.

The Bus to Rhossilli

While we're on the subject of writers on the Welsh coast, let's move down to south Wales and the scenic Gower Peninsula, which everyone thinks is glorious. Although Dylan Thomas thought his home town of Swansea 'ugly', he considered the nearby Gower Peninsula to be beautiful, and would often take the bus to Rhossilli on its western side, armed with a book and his lunch, and then walk along Worm's Head, where he'd spend all day reading.

Not that such halcyon pursuits didn't sometimes end in disaster. As Don Meredith notes in *Where the Tigers Were*, Thomas once fell asleep and got trapped out on Worm's Head by the incoming water, and couldn't head back onto the mainland until midnight, when he began the eighteen-mile walk back home to Swansea. During the long walk home, he experienced a series of hallucinations, including see-through ladies who vanished as he approached them. And this was *before* he began drinking eighteen straight whiskies.

The forename 'Dylan' was rare before David John 'Jack' Thomas, the poet's father, lifted it from relative obscurity among the pages of the *Mabinogion*, the book of Welsh legend, and gave it to his only son. All future boys named Dylan – to say nothing of Bob Dylan, who took his stage surname from the poet – owe him a debt for having done so. (Curiously, the Welsh pronunciation of the name is

'Dullan'; it was only because the poet grew up preferring 'Dillan' that the latter pronunciation became established.)

Thomas was a precocious talent. One of his earliest poems, 'The Mishap', is about a little boy who blew himself up. It isn't exactly a classic, but the poetry he produced in his late teenage years signalled the arrival of a new and distinctive voice in English poetry. Around half of his published poetic output was completed before he was twenty, while he was still living at home with his parents in Swansea. His first volume, *18 Poems*, was published shortly after his twentieth birthday.

Even his great radio drama, *Under Milk Wood*, which Thomas is thought to have begun in Oxfordshire and finished in the United States, had its origins in a play the seventeen-year-old Thomas had written for the school magazine, featuring nonsense dialogue between the Italian dictator Mussolini and his wife. (The name of the setting for *Under Milk Wood*, the fictional village of Llareggub, is 'bugger all' backwards, but nobody is quite sure whether Thomas had a particular town or village in mind.) Indeed, although he would spend a number of his brief adult years living in London, he would write only a handful of poems outside of his native Wales.

The Welsh Legends of Hergest

In 1849, a businesswoman and collector named Lady Charlotte Guest published her translation of a fourteenth-century collection of Welsh tales, often referred to as the *Red Book of Hergest*, under the Welsh title *The Mabinogion* (literally, 'story of youth'). The work was the product of over a decade's study, which had involved Guest learning Middle Welsh, the medieval Welsh language used in the Hergest manuscript, and talking to Welsh clerics about the language of the stories. The result was the first widely available English translation of Wales's foremost collection of myths. The *Mabinogion* contains some of Wales's finest mythical heroes, such as Bran the Blessed, the giant-king who, one imagines, had a huge beard and a very loud voice.

The *Red Book of Hergest* – so named because of its associations with Hergest Court, a fifteenth-century manor house on the Welsh borders – was almost certainly a revision of earlier versions of the tales, which had been in circulation both orally and in manuscript form for many centuries by the time the 'red book' was produced in the 1380s or shortly after. But such is the way with myths and legends, as the tales of King Arthur and Robin Hood attest. The real value of the Hergest manuscript, and the *Mabinogion*, resides in the stories themselves, and the way they show a Welsh literary tradition emerging through storytelling.

And talking of King Arthur, the British hero appears in the *Red Book of Hergest* – although it provides a very different portrait of that legendary king who is more familiar to us through the work of Geoffrey of Monmouth, Thomas Malory, Tennyson, and, of course, Monty Python. The Arthur we glimpse in the Hergest book is usually a marginal figure – such as in the tale of Peredur, son of Efrog, the Welsh version of the story of the knight Percival – but in 'The Dream of Rhonabwy', a decidedly odd tale in which the title character dreams he has travelled back to the time of King Arthur, we get a closer look at the warrior-king, as he sits playing gwyddbwyll (a Welsh board game vaguely resembling chess) with one of his followers shortly before the Battle of Badon. This curious story may not have originally been part of the *Mabinogion*, but when Guest added it to her translation of the *Red Book of Hergest*, it became a sort of orphan tale. Like the *Arabian Nights*, the *Mabinogion* grew up over time into the collection we now read.

The *Mabinogion* is worth reading for its tales of adventure and romance – not to mention its references to such fantastical things as invisibility cloaks, talking animals, giants, and shapeshifters. The stories in the *Mabinogion* were originally composed to be performed by bards and storytellers, and it shows. They're larger than life, like all good myths. But now, if you'll forgive me, I feel like lying down on a hill and having a nap . . .

Asleep in the Malvern Hills

In 1856, a book was published called *Three Weeks in Wet Sheets: A Moist Visitor to Malvern*. Reassuringly, it isn't about a faulty waterbed but rather the healing waters in the town. But Malvern is not just good for its spa water. Apparently it's also a good place for a dream, or at least it is if you're a fourteenth-century English poet, which I'm assuming you're not. But in case you feel as though you may have been one in a past life, you may be interested to learn that lying between Herefordshire and Worcestershire are the Malvern Hills, which provide the setting for the beginning of William Langland's poem *Piers Plowman*, composed some time in the second half of the fourteenth century. (The name Malvern, by the way, is thought to derive from the ancient British *moel-bryn*, meaning 'bare hill', so the Malvern Hills are literally the 'bare hill hills'.) It was here that the poet fell asleep in one of the greatest and most popular poems of the entire Middle Ages:

Ac on a May morwenynge on Malverne hilles
Me bifel a ferly, of Fairye me thoghte.

In other words, 'But on a May morning on the Malvern hills, a marvel befell me, of fairy methought.' The ensuing poem tells, in unrhymed alliterative verse, of the dreams the poet experienced (contrary to popular belief, Piers

Plowman is one of the figures who appear in the dreams, not the dreamer himself), which focus on a quest for personal salvation, corruption in the Church, and the value of the human heart over the power of cold intellect. What he had for his lunch is not recorded.

Who Langland was remains something of a mystery. The one clinching piece of evidence we have for his authorship of the poem is an early fifteenth-century manuscript which names him as the son of an Oxfordshire man, Stacy de Rokayle, and as the one who 'made the book which is called *Piers Plowman*'. From internal clues offered in the poem, it appears he was tall – the 'Lang' of 'Langland' means 'long' – and was from the Malvern area, a fact revealed through the poem's dialect. It's also possible that the poet was educated at the priory at Great Malvern, built soon after the Norman Conquest and now a parish church. But beyond this, much of the biography of Langland is composed of guesswork and hunches. We don't even know for sure if 'William Langland' was his real name. A William Rokele was initiated into the clergy in the late 1330s and may, in light of the surname of the poet's father, have been the man we know as William Langland, with 'Langland' being more of a nickname. The problem is that we have so little to go on. Unlike his contemporary Geoffrey Chaucer, who worked at the royal court and about whom extensive records were kept, Langland is a cipher and little more.

Although the name William Langland remains something of an enigma, it's clear that Piers Plowman became an instantly recognisable name throughout medieval England. John Ball, the priest of the Peasants' Revolt of 1381, mentioned the character in a letter of the same year.

The poem offers the earliest known reference to the figure of Robin Hood, when a drunken priest named Sloth boasts that he knows the 'rymes of Robyn Hood, and Randolf erle of Chestre' (evidently the rhymes about Randolf, or Ranulf, haven't weathered so agreeably as those featuring Robin Hood).

And although the Malvern landscape is mentioned only a handful of times in this long poem, its position is arguably central to the poem's exploration of the individual Christian's simple existence, such as here in the Worcestershire countryside, contrasted with the power of religious institutions based in the bigger towns and cities.

Remembering Adlestrop

If things had been different, Edward Thomas might have written a poem called 'Titlestrop'.

The origins of Thomas's most famous poem lie in an event that took place on 24 June 1914, while the poet was on the Oxford to Worcester express train. The train made an unscheduled stop at Adlestrop (which is listed as Titlestrop in the *Domesday Book*) in Gloucestershire, a tiny village in the Cotswolds with a population of just over 100. (Well, Thomas himself refers to the stop as 'unscheduled', but the time of his sojourn there, 12.45, corresponds to a scheduled stopping service. But poetic licence and all that . . .) While the train was stationary at Adlestrop, Thomas took the opportunity to fill his notebook with his observations of the place – he was a prolific keeper of nature journals – before the train started up again. The poem, then, had its origins in an unexpected event, a chance occurrence, that occurred one summer's day in 1914.

Adlestrop is now inextricably associated with Thomas's poem, but he wasn't the first famous writer to go there. Jane Austen visited the former rectory at Adlestrop three times – her mother's cousin lived there – and Mansfield Park in her novel of that name may have been partly inspired by her visits to Adlestrop House.

I say 'an event' took place that day in 1914, but really the secret of Thomas's poem lies in the singular uneventfulness of what it describes. Part of the reason the poem appeals to readers, I would venture, is its typically British understatedness: it describes the beauty of the English countryside and the flora and fauna there (Thomas, as well as being a poet, was also a very good nature writer) in very matter-of-fact terms. Note, too, the specificity of the detail: 'meadowsweet' is mead wort, a herb that is found in damp meadows. It's Wordsworth with all the 'egotistical sublime' (to borrow Keats's phrase) removed, and the emotional engagement reined in tightly.

Thomas had taken up poetry relatively late in life, having tried his hand at being a reviewer and critic. It was the American poet Robert Frost who encouraged him to give poetry a go. Frost, who saw something in the largely unknown Thomas, then in his mid thirties, said wittily that Thomas's problem was that he 'was suffering from a life of insubordination to his inferiors'. Indeed, Edward Thomas was on his way to Robert Frost's home near Ledbury on that momentous day 'in late June' when his train made that unexpected stop at Adlestrop.

One of the other reasons for the poem's popularity lies in the date on which that unscheduled stop occurred. 24 June 1914 is just a few weeks before the outbreak of the First World War. Like Rupert Brooke's 'The Old Vicarage, Grantchester', 'Adlestrop' describes the England of sunny innocence before August 1914, when the First World War changed everything. The train, a symbol of modernity and movement, stops and allows Thomas, too, to stop, pause, contemplate, observe, and admire the surroundings. The increasingly busy and fast-moving world suddenly slows right down to allow a brief moment – 'that minute' – in which to enjoy nature and stillness, peace and beauty. This is, suddenly, a world of stillness and slowness again, not the bustling modern world: 'No one left and no one came / On the bare platform'.

The First World War would change poetry, too, with the style and world-view of the Georgian poets (with whom Thomas was associated) soon being challenged by modernists like T. S. Eliot and Ezra Pound. Thomas himself would be killed in 1917; he never lived to see 'Adlestrop' published.

There isn't a railway station at Adlestrop any more. It was closed in 1966 during the Beeching cuts. But the poem is inscribed on the bench that occupies the place where the station could be found, all those years ago during that magical minute in June.

The Imaginary Monk of Bristol

Of all the places in Britain that might be considered the birthplace of English Romanticism, Bristol is probably not near the top of most people's lists.

Yet William Wordsworth completed 'Lines Written a Few Miles above Tintern Abbey' in the parlour of his publisher, Joseph Cottle, in Bristol. He may have begun writing his lines in the Wye valley, but he was deep in the city when he put the finishing touches to his famous verse meditation on the self, the countryside, and the gathering of wisdom with time.

But Bristol's Romantic links predate Wordsworth. Thomas Hardy wrote in *A Pair of Blue Eyes* that 'Stratford has her Shakespeare' and 'Bristol has her Chatterton'. Thomas Chatterton (1752–70) was arguably the first English Romantic poet; before Wordsworth was even born (he died the year young William came into the world), it was Chatterton who was laying the groundwork for a revolution in English verse. He was also, perhaps, the most precocious English poet who has ever lived – despite being dismissed from one school for being, in the words of his writing master, 'a dull boy, and incapable of improvement'.

Chatterton's mother and sister taught him to read before he won a place at Colston's, Bristol's 'bluecoat' school, founded by a charitable local merchant. He soon got the reading bug and had his nose in a book at every opportunity, often reading among the tombs in St Mary Redcliffe, a church not far from where Bristol Temple Meads station now stands. His earliest surviving poems were written in January 1764 when he was just eleven years old. He soon fell in love with all things medieval – and then Chatterton revealed that he had discovered the works of Thomas Rowley, a medieval poet, priest, and friend of William Canynge, who had been mayor of Bristol in the mid fifteenth century. Stylistically, Rowley's poetry is a mixture of Middle English ballads and Chaucerian language, with the poems bearing such medieval-sounding titles as 'Ælla' and 'The Parlyamente of Sprytes'.

In reality, there was no Thomas Rowley. The poet-priest was entirely Chatterton's invention, though he almost certainly took the name from a brass tablet in St John's Gate church in Bristol. Chatterton wrote a considerable number of Rowley poems, and even succeeded in passing them off as genuine medieval poems . . . for a while, at least. He managed to convince a number of high-profile readers, including the Lord Mayor of London, William Beckford, father of the Gothic novelist of the same name, and even fooled some of the literary greats of the day – including Horace Walpole, the author of the first Gothic novel, *The Castle of Otranto*. At least, initially – but the more Walpole read, the more he smelled a rat, until he eventually withdrew his offer to publish the poems, having realised they were forgeries. This is especially apt given that *The Castle of Otranto* was itself offered to the public on its original publication in 1764 as a genuine medieval manuscript, until Walpole came clean in the reprinted version a year later. The old adage is true: it really does take one to know one.

Chatterton might have gone on to be one of the leading

lights in English Romantic poetry, but he took his own life, aged just seventeen. Travelling to London in the hope of finding financial recognition there, he failed to make a living as a writer, and in August 1770 he committed suicide by poison – a phial of arsenic – in his Holborn flat. At the time, Wordsworth was just a babe in arms, at four months old, and English Romantic poetry would have to wait nearly a quarter of a century before Chatterton's legacy truly grew. His death would be immortalised in a painting of 1856; the sitter for the portrait was none other than the Victorian poet and novelist, George Meredith.

Chatterton was also immortalised by later poets as the patron saint of the Romantic movement. Wordsworth called him the 'marvellous boy'. Coleridge's first published poem was about him. The Pre-Raphaelite poet and artist Dante Gabriel Rossetti considered him the equal to Shakespeare. And then the Victorian poet Robert Browning borrowed the word 'slug-horn' from Chatterton's pseudo-medieval poetry for his famous 1855 pseudo-medieval poem 'Childe Roland to the Dark Tower Came'. Even more recently, J. K. Rowling has put the slug-horn to new use, in the name of Horace Slughorn, a character from the *Harry Potter* series.

Folly at Fonthill Abbey

The Gothic novelist William Beckford – son of the Lord Mayor of London, who was taken in by Chatterton's medieval forgeries – was mad about porcelain, though perhaps we can lose the words 'about porcelain'. He was certainly eccentric. At the age of nineteen, he wrote of walking 'in arched Chambers glowing with yellow Light – amidst Vases formed in another Hemisphere – and cabalistic Mirrors wherein Futurity is unveiled'. It was, in a sense, his vision for the ultimate home – and a house he would later build, with calamitous consequences.

Beckford had wealth – he was heir to a mighty sugar empire in the West Indies, and Byron described him as 'England's wealthiest son' in his poem *Childe Harold's Pilgrimage* – but, thanks to an unfortunate event in 1784, he was to spend the rest of his life as something of a social outcast. The rumour is that he was caught *in flagrante delicto* with a beautiful youth, William Courtenay. Precisely what occurred is difficult to say. The diarist Joseph Farington, who heard the story at second or even third hand, recorded that somebody walked in on Beckford and Courtenay in the latter's bedroom, and 'Courtenay was discovered in his shirt, and Beckford in some posture or other – Strange story'. Whatever Beckford's 'posture' had been at this moment of unexpected exposure – and it's tempting to surmise that while Courtenay was discovered in his shirt, Beckford was discovered in Courtenay's trousers – the story damaged Beckford's reputation permanently, and he was to find himself shut off from all of the advantages he might otherwise have expected to enjoy, such as a peerage or the respect of the people.

Throughout his life, Beckford found solace in books. In the 1790s, he bought Edward Gibbon's entire library for £950, simply so he would have 'something to read when I passed through Lausanne'. He later recalled how he 'shut myself up for six weeks from early in the morning until night . . . The people thought me mad. I read myself nearly blind'. His literary significance rests on *Vathek*, a short Gothic novel which he wrote when he was still in his early twenties. Beckford wrote it in French and left it to a scholar named Samuel Henley to translate into English, with the English version being published first. (Jorge Luis Borges memorably quipped that the original was unfaithful to the translation.) The novel is about the titular Caliph who devotes his life to the pursuit of pleasure, and builds five luxurious palaces – one for each of the five senses – in order to help him in his hedonistic quest. It was one of the earliest Gothic novels and helped to create the genre, along with Horace Walpole's *The Castle of Otranto*.

Unlike Vathek, Beckford would build only one palace: the Gothic pile named Fonthill Abbey, although the construction of the building ended up being rushed, such was Beckford's impatience to move in. He invited a young J. M. W. Turner to come down and paint a picture of the abbey, but the view from the outside concealed a multitude of architectural sins on the inside. Thirteen of its eighteen bedrooms remained empty, because they were too cold and damp to be habitable. As Anita McConnell observes in the *Oxford Dictionary of National Biography*, Beckford appeared to have given more thought to accommodating himself when dead than while he was still alive. Yet visitors loved it. Not that it was a good idea to take a trip down to Wiltshire to see it: Beckford installed fierce dogs and a fair number of man-traps on the grounds, and built a 7-mile wall that stood 12 feet (3.6 metres) high, designed to keep foxhunters (whom Beckford especially loathed) out of his grounds. Keeping watch at the gate was a 'malodorous' dwarf from Switzerland named Perro, who stood there dressed in a gold suit keeping the commoners, and anyone else Beckford didn't like, out.

In 1825, Fonthill Tower, which stood 276 feet (84 metres) tall, collapsed, taking much of the western hall with it. When Beckford had to sell the house, the Irish poet Thomas Moore, who was staying at lodgings nearby, wandered over to see Beckford's belongings being sold off, and bought a cup and saucer for his wife. At least his beloved porcelain went to a good literary home.

Writing Stonehenge

When J. M. W. Turner was on his way to Fonthill Abbey – or, possibly, on his way back from it – he stopped and observed Stonehenge, the bewitching and enigmatic stone circle on Salisbury Plain, which he would later paint on several occasions. Stonehenge has attracted endless speculation from writers – indeed, from pretty much everyone. The twelfth-century historian Geoffrey of Monmouth believed that King Arthur's magician Merlin had been responsible for it, and that Arthur's father Uther Pendragon, and the legendary king Constantine, had both been buried there. In the nineteenth century, Thomas Hardy drew on the site's pagan associations for his novel *Tess of the d'Urbervilles*: his heroine, on the run after murdering Alec d'Urberville, is apprehended here and subsequently taken off for trial and execution. It's as if Tess is a modern-day sacrifice being offered up to the gods.

But it was in the seventeenth century that the most important link between literature and Stonehenge was forged. John Aubrey (who lived at the nearby Old Rectory at Broad Chalke, the Wiltshire village where Terry Pratchett would live 300 years later) was a remarkable figure: writer, biographer, antiquary, and natural philosopher (what we'd nowadays call a scientist). His *Brief Lives*, a collection of short sketches about the great and good of the sixteenth and seventeenth centuries, is essentially the first English work of biography – a word which arrived in the language at this time.

But Aubrey's interests ranged far and wide, and he found his curiosity was especially piqued by the ancient stone circles at nearby Avebury and Stonehenge. Aubrey wasn't the first person to identify the site at Avebury: an Elizabethan antiquarian named William Camden had written about the village and the standing stones, but failed to note their significance. Aubrey first encountered the site while out hunting in 1649 and was 'wonderfully surprised at the sight of those vast stones of which I had never heard before'. He was the first person to realise that Avebury and Stonehenge predated not only the Vikings or Saxons, but the Roman presence in Britain too – in short, that they were thousands of years older than previously believed. Aubrey later told King Charles II about the site, and in 1663 the King insisted on riding out from Bath with Aubrey to visit it. (While there, Charles climbed nearby Silbury Hill, the vast Neolithic mound which Aubrey also kept detailed notes on.)

All this happened at just the right time. Avebury was being plundered and gradually dismantled by locals, who didn't share the antiquarian's interest in historical study. Many of them – Puritans, on the whole – took a dislike to the standing stones for religious reasons, denouncing them as pagan idols that needed to be torn down. Thankfully, Aubrey had made extensive notes about Avebury before too much of the site was demolished, although, like so much of his work, his writings on Avebury were only discovered, and their importance realised, long after his death. He compiled his research into a document named *Monumenta Britannica*, but it wouldn't be published until 1980, when it was co-edited by the novelist John Fowles.

After Avebury, Aubrey turned his attention to Stonehenge, where in 1666 he discovered five circular cavities in the ground. In the 1920s, an archaeologist would name a series of similar depressions on the site 'Aubrey holes' in his honour – confusingly, though, the ones named after him were almost certainly not the same ones that Aubrey himself had noticed. Nevertheless, the name nicely commemorates Aubrey's early interest in the site and his desire to preserve and understand it for its historical importance.

John Aubrey was a pioneering figure in the history of biography, but the writer and archaeologist Aubrey Burl has also called him 'Britain's first archaeologist'. His interest in antiquities of all kinds would benefit posterity in innumerable ways. As Aubrey himself put it in one of his *Brief Lives*, 'How these curiosities would be quite forgott, did not such idle fellowes as I am putt them downe.' We know more about Avebury and Stonehenge because he bothered to do so.

Selborne, Naturally

What was the bestselling book in Britain in the eighteenth century? One candidate is Gilbert White's *The Natural History and Antiquities of Selborne* (1789), which originated in a series of letters White sent to other naturalists of the age. The book has gone through 300 editions and has been admired by everyone from Samuel Taylor Coleridge and Charles Darwin to Virginia Woolf and W. H. Auden. It's been claimed (though it's impossible to ascertain, given the shaky record of sales figures in the eighteenth and nineteenth centuries) that White's book is the fourth biggest-selling book in English, after the King James Bible, the works of Shakespeare, and *The Pilgrim's Progress*. However you look at it, White became a publishing phenomenon and his *Natural History* became the must-have book on the natural world.

White is often called the first ecologist and the first environmentalist, words that wouldn't come into being until over a century after his death. The naturalist Stephen Moss has also suggested that White was the father of bird-watching in England, a pastime that would only become truly popular in the twentieth century. (It did exist in the nineteenth century, but often involved a gun rather than a pair of binoculars, with the express aim being to shoot the bird on sight, then take it home, stuff it and eat it.) It would be difficult to overstate his importance in the field of nature studies. And he became Britain's leading naturalist from his home in the small village of Selborne in Hampshire, where he was curate.

In 1751, White began keeping his *Garden Kalendar*, an extensive record of the local environment around Selborne covering everything from the life cycles of invertebrates to the mating habits of the animals in the region. The *Kalendar* was effectively one long nature diary, which White updated virtually every day for the next forty years until shortly before his death. (Among other things, he's particularly interested in keeping the reader up to speed with his cucumbers, and how many he's harvested that day.) White also became interested in growing melons – not an easy thing to do in the English climate – which involved cultivating a 45-feet (14-metre) long 'hot bed' and the regular application of '18 good dung-carts of fresh, hot dung', as his *Garden Kalendar* heartily records.

White became the 'go-to guy' among late eighteenth-century naturalists and amateur botanists, with his encyclopedic brain being picked by the great and good of the age. It was this correspondence with other naturalists which formed the basis of *The Natural History of Selborne*. White's letters would also have another, more surprising, legacy: he was the first person known to use an 'x' to represent a kiss, in a letter of 1763. Quite why he chose this symbol, nobody really knows, though one theory has it that it's related to the custom of using 'X' as a shorthand for Christ. Why Christ should then suggest kisses in letters isn't entirely clear, and a rival theory – that the tradition arose out of illiterate people's practice of signing documents with an 'X' – is perhaps more likely. Whatever its origins, White's innovation would eventually take off. Another early adopter of the 'x' as a kiss was Winston

Churchill, who signed off a letter of 1894 with the words, 'Please excuse bad writing as I am in an awful hurry. (Many kisses.) xxx WSC.'

Selborne has remained largely unaltered since White's time, over two centuries ago. Around four miles from Selborne is Chawton, the home of the Jane Austen Museum – and it is to Jane Austen that we now turn.

Two Poems from Winchester

Winchester Cathedral library is the oldest book room in Europe, dating from the twelfth century. Treasures include the Winchester Bible, dating from around 1150, and Sir Walter Ralegh's speech from the scaffold in 1618. But Winchester has also played host to a number of distinguished literary visitors. In the early nineteenth century, two literary giants of the age wrote poems at Winchester. One poem would become a classic – one of the most famous in the language – while the other would sink into obscurity, although it was written by one of the most celebrated writers of the age.

Probably the most famous person buried in Winchester Cathedral is Jane Austen, who died in the city in 1817. Three days before her death, Austen wrote a poem about the city, 'Venta' (the Latin for Winchester), a light-hearted verse celebrating the city's saint, Swithun:

When Winchester races first took their beginning
It is said the good people forgot their old Saint
Not applying at all for the leave of Saint Swithin
And that William of Wykeham's approval was faint.

The races however were fixed and determined
The company came and the Weather was charming
The Lords and the Ladies were satin'd and ermin'd
And nobody saw any future alarming.

But when the old Saint was informed of these doings
He made but one spring from his shrine to the roof
Of the Palace which now lies so sadly in ruins
And then he address'd them all standing aloof.

Oh, subjects rebellious, Oh Venta depraved
When once we are buried you think we are dead
But behold me Immortal. – By vice you're enslaved
You have sinn'd and must suffer. – Then farther he said

These races and revels and dissolute measures
With which you're debasing a neighbouring Plain
Let them stand – you shall meet with your curse in your
pleasures
Set off for your course, I'll pursue with my rain.

Ye cannot but know my command o'er July
Henceforward I'll triumph in shewing my powers,
Shift your race as you will it shall never be dry
The curse upon Venta is July in showers.

The poem contains the same satiric spirit which informs
Austen's novels, gently mocking the people of Winchester
for going to the races on their city's saint's day. The poem
was allowed to languish in manuscript form until 1906,
when it was finally published.

Austen isn't celebrated for her poems, of course. But a
couple of years after she penned her light verse to the city,
in 1819, Keats visited Winchester with Charles Armitage,
and wrote 'To Autumn' during his stay here. He left the
city in early October, but by that time he'd written one
of his greatest poems. 'I take a walk every day for an hour

before dinner and this is generally my walk', he wrote in a letter:

> I go out at the back gate across one street, into the Cathedral yard, along a paved path, past the beautiful front of the Cathedral, turn to the left under a stone doorway – then I am on the other side of the building – which leaving behind me I pass on through two college-like squares seemingly built for the dwelling place of Deans and Prebendaries – garnished with grass and shaded with trees. Then I pass through one of the old city gates and then you are in College Street.

And there 'you', indeed, can be to this day, if you follow Keats's walking suggestions. But we cannot tarry in Winchester any longer: there's an altercation in William Blake's garden, and it's all threatening to kick off.

A Poet on Trial in Chichester

From Winchester we travel along to Chichester, where Keats also stayed in 1819. It's thought he started writing 'The Eve of St Agnes' during his visit, and was quite possibly inspired by the medieval architecture of Chichester while composing the poem.

Sixteen years earlier, in 1803, another Romantic poet was having a very different time in Chichester. A disagreement in his garden led to William Blake being put on trial for sedition. Blake was a controversial figure, but even so, 'seditious' seems perhaps a bit strong. It all started when the poet and engraver found a soldier in his garden.

These were dangerous times. War with France had just been renewed, and Blake was known to be highly critical of the British army. In August 1803, the ostler from the local pub was doing some gardening for Blake in his cottage garden in the nearby village of Felpham. The ostler had enlisted the help of a soldier, John Scofield, but hadn't mentioned this to Blake. When Blake found the soldier lounging around in his garden, seemingly drunk and disorderly, he saw red and went out to confront the hapless man. Scofield refused to leave.

Blake was not a big man, and the soldier was, by all accounts, large and lumbering. Nevertheless, as Alexander Gilchrist quaintly put it in his *Life of William Blake*, the poet 'turned him out neck and crop, in a kind of inspired frenzy, which took the man aback, and fairly frightened him'. Blake then frogmarched the soldier back to the local pub, the Fox Inn, before returning home to his now soldierless garden. He was surprised a few days later to learn that he had been accused of sedition, for supposedly damning the king while he'd been escorting the drunken redcoat back to the inn.

The trial took place in January 1804, at Chichester's Guildhall. As the charges were read out and the case was launched against him, Blake is said to have yelled 'False!' in response to each of the charges, which was actually more effective as a method of legal defence than one might expect. He was duly acquitted, and that was the end of it. But it's curious that the one thing that landed Blake in trouble for sedition was nothing that he wrote or published, but something he said – or, as it turns out, never said.

Garibaldi at Farringford

Blake may have been found innocent of sedition, but one connection between poetry and political revolution can be found on the Isle of Wight.

Alfred, Lord Tennyson had a slow start making his name as a poet. His first published volume of poems was a collection, *Poems by Two Brothers*, which appeared in 1827 when Alfred was still a teenager. The volume was actually the work of three brothers: Alfred, Frederick, and Charles. It didn't bode well for the book's fortunes that the siblings couldn't even get the title right and agree on how many of them had written it.

Then, three years later, Alfred went solo with *Poems, Chiefly Lyrical*, which introduced the phrase 'airy-fairy' into the language (in the poem 'Lilian') and contained one of Tennyson's finest poems, 'Mariana', but was otherwise fairly unremarkable. Another volume followed three years later, but the critical panning it received, along with the sudden death of Tennyson's close university friend Arthur Hallam, caused the young poet to retreat into the shadows for nearly a decade. His *annus mirabilis* eventually came in 1850, when his long elegy for Hallam, *In Memoriam*, was published, and Tennyson was appointed Poet Laureate following Wordsworth's death. Oh, and he got married.

Tennyson subsequently attained considerable fame and fortune. He was perhaps the last true celebrity poet in Britain; nobody in the twentieth century, except perhaps

Betjeman, came close. Tennyson and his family retreated from mainland Britain to the Isle of Wight, where he set up a home, Farringford, on the west side of the island. The Tennysons' many distinguished visitors to Farringford included the poets Arthur Hugh Clough, Edward Lear, and Algernon Charles Swinburne, the novelist Charles Kingsley, and even a Hawaiian queen – Queen Emma of the Sandwich Islands, whom Tennyson hid from his other guests 'among the cabbages' in the summer house so that she might read her letters in peace.

But perhaps the most famous guest Tennyson entertained at Farringford was Giuseppe Garibaldi, when the Italian general visited Britain in 1864. Tennyson's wife Emily left a record of Garibaldi's visit in her journal, stating that he was 'a most striking figure' whose face was 'very noble' and 'powerful' but also 'sweet'. Tennyson and Garibaldi went and talked politics in the poet's study, and Tennyson warned the general not to talk politics in England, which is as good a piece of advice now as it was then. Garibaldi admired the poet's primroses, and the two men planted a tree together. Before long the Italian revolutionary had set off for the mainland, and that was the end of a brief and unlikely meeting between Britain's foremost poet of the age and Italy's leading general.

Hardy's Wessex?

We rejoin the mainland further along the coast at Dorset, or, to use the literary terminology, 'Hardy's Wessex'. Which is fitting given that Hardy admired Tennyson's work and Tennyson, by all accounts, returned the compliment.

The name 'Wessex' is bound up with history, but in all sorts of ways it is a peculiarly literary history. It was Thomas Hardy who revived the old Anglo-Saxon name for the West Country – literally, the land of the West Saxons – when he invented a fictionalised landscape, 'partly real, partly dream-country' as he put it, in which Dorchester became Casterbridge, Salisbury became Melchester, and the Isle of Wight became 'The Island' (some of his names were more inventive than others).

Well, actually it wasn't Hardy who revived this old name at all. This is something of a misconception. In blowing the dust off the name 'Wessex', Hardy was following the lead of his mentor and fellow Dorset poet William Barnes (1801–86). But then you'd be surprised how often Hardy gets the credit for Barnes's achievements. When I was down in Dorchester in 2016, Google Maps directed me to Thomas Hardy's statue on the High Street. Following the directions, I was surprised to find myself looking up at what could only be described as a statue of William Barnes.

Barnes was a remarkable man. Although he went to Cambridge and received a degree in divinity, he was largely self-taught when it came to everything else, training himself in mathematics and music and becoming fluent in seven languages. He wrote poems in the Dorset dialect, and thought the Latinate and Romance influence on the English language should be rolled back in favour of Anglo-Saxon formations. People shouldn't ride bicycles, he said, but 'wheelsaddles'. Similarly, you don't get on the bus but the 'folkwain'. 'Leechcraft', he suggested somewhat improbably, was preferable to medicine. Perhaps his boldest suggestion was that forceps should be referred to as 'nipperlings', a recommendation that medical professionals haven't rushed to put into practice.

Yet Barnes's fondness for the perceived purity of Old English terms explains why it was he, not Hardy, who first resurrected the Saxon term 'Wessex' for the area of England which he held so dear. As he put it in the 1868 preface to a volume of his poems, 'As I think that some people, beyond the bounds of Wessex, would allow me the pleasure of believing that they have deemed . . . my homely poems in our Dorset mother-speech to be worthy of their reading, I have written a few of a like kind, in common English.' Hardy would take up the name six years later, in his novel *Far from the Madding Crowd*. He would even name his dog Wessex, and immortalised the animal in 'A Popular Personage at Home' – a poem in which Hardy allows 'Wessex' to speak for himself.

Sticking with all things Wessex, the title Earl of Wessex also died out only to be resurrected much later – and here, too, we may have a writer to thank for its return: William Shakespeare. Or perhaps that should be Tom Stoppard. You see, the most famous medieval Earl of Wessex died at the Battle of Hastings in 1066, when, according to the leading theory, he copped an arrow in the eye. Harold II of England (as he's more familiarly known) died at Hastings and his title was passed to William FitzOsbern, one of William the Conqueror's Norman knights. When FitzOsbern died five years later, the title disappeared from history.

That is, until 1999, when it was dusted off and given to the Queen's youngest son, Prince Edward, upon his marriage to Sophie Rhys-Jones. According to one royal courtier, the title Earl of Wessex was chosen because it had featured in the 1998 film *Shakespeare in Love*, whose screenplay was co-written by the playwright Tom Stoppard. In the film, Colin Firth plays the earl – a piece of flagrant anachronism, given that during the period when the play is set the last holder of the title had been dead for over five centuries. But rumour has it that the prince enjoyed the film, so he was given the Earldom of Wessex. The other leading candidate in the box of royal titles, Duke of Cambridge, was shelved until Prince William married in 2011.

My Heart is in Stinsford

In the Dorset village of Stinsford, about a mile east of Dorchester, you can find the grave of Thomas Hardy (1840–1928). Or rather, you both can and can't find it there. This is because whilst there is a gravestone to Thomas Hardy in Stinsford churchyard, he isn't there – although, in a very literal sense, his heart's in the right place.

I went and visited Hardy's grave on a hot summer's day, trekking from Dorchester town centre out to the small village church of Stinsford, which appears as Mellstock in Hardy's writing. It was something of an impromptu pilgrimage. Had I done my research before I'd set off, I could also have sought out the final resting place of Cecil Day-Lewis (Poet Laureate between 1968 and 1972 and the father of the actor Daniel Day-Lewis), who wished to be buried in the same churchyard as his literary hero. That I managed to find Hardy's grave was lucky enough. It looks much like any other in this rather typical village churchyard. But what's intriguing about the grave is the inscription: 'Here lies the heart of Thomas Hardy'. Where's the rest of him, then?

Thomas Hardy had become a literary institution by the time he died, aged eighty-seven, in 1928. Although he'd abandoned novel writing back in the 1890s, he went on composing poems to the end – indeed, he dictated his last poem to his second wife while on his deathbed. Hardy wanted to be buried in his beloved Dorset next to his first wife, Emma, but his executor, a man who bore the magnificent name of Sir Sydney Carlyle Cockerell, had other ideas. Hardy was too important a writer to be hidden away down in some obscure graveyard in the West Country; he should be laid to rest in Poets' Corner alongside Chaucer and Spenser and Dickens and the other literary immortals. A compromise was reached: Hardy would be buried in Westminster Abbey but his heart would be removed from his body and interred in Stinsford next to Emma.

The list of Hardy's pall-bearers at his funeral in Westminster Abbey reads like a roll-call of the literary and political establishment of the day: Rudyard Kipling, George Bernard Shaw, John Galsworthy, A. E. Housman, J. M. Barrie, Edmund Gosse, the leader of the Opposition, and even the prime minister, Stanley Baldwin. The heart-burying ceremony down in Stinsford attracted less illustrious names, but then it hardly required such literary titans to carry the small casket in which Hardy's heart was contained. The ceremony was, however, committed to film by British Pathé – you can find the footage online.

Hardy was a rural writer and he remained so, despite the literary recognition he received in his later years. For much of his life he would spend half the year in London, pressured by his wife Emma into being part of the literary scene, but he refused to leave his beloved Dorset altogether, and he wrote his best work here; the novels he wrote while in London are now his least read. And although he was a 'village atheist' (in the words of G. K. Chesterton), he retained an interest in local rustic superstitions and customs, which he explored in his ghostly short story 'The Withered Arm'. (He also believed, altogether more oddly, that the reason the trees outside his house didn't thrive was that he looked at them before breakfast on an empty stomach.) Hardy was a believer in what he called 'life's little ironies'. 'All comedy is tragedy, if you only look deep enough into it,' he opined in a letter to John Addington Symonds in 1889. Indeed, his novels would take a more tragic turn as his career developed.

Hardy's life carried a tragicomic vein from the start. He was born in Stinsford, in the area known then as Upper Bockhampton, in June 1840 – although he was presumed stillborn until an eagle-eyed midwife spotted that the baby was, in fact, not dead. And his death was shot through with irony, too – or rather, what happened after his death. For there's a rumour that Hardy's heart isn't really in the Stinsford grave. The story goes that while that organ was awaiting burial, a hungry cat came across the heart and ate it. The rumour appears to have no basis in fact, however, so if you visit Hardy's grave in Stinsford, you can be pretty sure he's there – or part of him was interred there, at any rate.

The Hardy Monument near Weymouth is often assumed to commemorate Thomas Hardy, and it does – but not the writer Thomas Hardy. Instead, the monument memorialises Vice Admiral Thomas Hardy, a commander at the Battle of Trafalgar – the one whom Nelson, in his dying moments, wanted to kiss.

Fantastic Bournemouth

In Hardy's Wessex, the Dorset seaside town of Bournemouth became Sandbourne, but we begin the next stop on our literary odyssey in another sandy place, Sandfield Road. Which doesn't sound especially exciting, though it just so happens it was the home of the author of the most popular fantasy novel ever written. For it was on Sandfield Road in Oxford that fantasy fans could visit their hero, J. R. R. Tolkien.

Not that Tolkien necessarily wanted them to visit, if that meant turning up unannounced. Tolkien had lived in his modest-sized home in Headington since 1953, but in the 1960s, as *The Lord of the Rings* started to take off in the United States, admirers began to turn up on the author's doorstep asking to have their books signed. Some even called him up, which was irritating enough when the caller was from the UK, but when enthusiasts from the United States started ringing at all hours, failing to acknowledge there was a time-zone difference, Tolkien and his wife, Edith, decided to leave Oxford and move to Dorset, where they had spent many happy holidays. (Lyme Regis was a favourite of Tolkien's: when he visited the Philpot Museum there, he was struck by the 'petrified dragons', i.e. the dinosaur fossils.)

Oddly, W. H. Auden had done his bit to make life in Oxford unbearable – indeed, virtually untenable – for Tolkien by the late 1960s. In 1966, Auden, a fan and champion of Tolkien's work, told a room of New York fans at the Tolkien Society of America that their idol lived in a 'hideous house' with 'hideous pictures'. Many Americans turned up in the hope of finding out just *how* hideous their literary hero's own Hobbit hole really was.

Tolkien relocated to Bournemouth – well, technically, nearby Poole – in 1968, when he and Edith moved into a small bungalow on Lakeside Road. The move was as much for his wife's peace of mind as his own. She had grown weary of his celebrity status, and Tolkien made sure that Auden – and everyone else – kept his address secret this time, with all of his fan mail going to his publisher. While he lived out his last few years here, he continued to write, beavering away at his life's work, *The Silmarillion*. But in 1971 Edith died and Tolkien decided to move back to Oxford, taking up Merton College's offer of a live-in fellowship which meant that he could essentially revert to undergraduate life, sleeping in college rooms with meals provided and all his cleaning done for him. However, it was in Bournemouth that he died two years later, after he was taken ill while visiting friends down in Dorset.

Tolkien fans cannot make their pilgrimage to his Poole home, because it was demolished in 2008 and replaced with two energy-efficient luxury houses. But Tolkien's time in Dorset is a reminder of how he became an unlikely literary celebrity for millions of fans around the world. If that had never happened, he would have remained in Oxford.

Romantics at Nether Stowey

Tolkien in Dorset (rather than Oxford) raises an intriguing question about writers and the locations with which they are most closely associated. If you had to play a game in which you matched a writer to the place they were most associated with, it would be easy in some cases. Dickens and London. Hardy and Dorset. Wordsworth and the Lake District.

Yet the last of these tends to obscure the importance of Somerset to the birth of the English Romantic movement. Wordsworth and Coleridge first met each other in Bristol in 1795, and as we've already seen, it was in Bristol that the proto-Romantic poet, Thomas Chatterton, was born and raised. Coleridge, who had been born in the wonderfully named village of Ottery St Mary in Devon in 1772, retained a distinctive West Country accent all his life. In 1796, he and his wife Sara moved to a small cottage – which was, by all accounts, filled with damp and overrun by mice – in Nether Stowey, a village near the Quantocks. Perhaps 'the hovel', as Coleridge affectionately referred to it, was as important to the formation of English Romanticism as Dove Cottage some 300 miles away. Indeed, it was probably more so. Even a director of the Wordsworth Trust, Dr Robert Woof, observed that whilst he felt the West Country connection didn't tell the full story, the time Wordsworth and Coleridge spent in Somerset was perhaps the most 'vital vortex' in English literature.

Was Somerset as important for the writing of the *Lyrical Ballads* as Grasmere? Coleridge wrote *The Rime of the Ancient Mariner* here, inspired by local man John Cruikshank's story of a dream he'd had about a skeleton ship manned by phantom sailors. (It was Wordsworth who suggested the curse – namely, that the shooting of an albatross brings bad luck to a ship's crew.) Perhaps inevitably, there's a pub here named in honour of Coleridge's poem. At the nearby harbour of Watchet – from which the Ancient Mariner sets off for his voyage – there's a statue commemorating the character. Despite the poem's later reputation as one of the defining poems in *Lyrical Ballads*, Wordsworth was displeased with its inclusion in the volume, and thought it put readers off; he even toyed with taking it out of subsequent editions and replacing it with 'some little things which would be more likely to suit the common taste'. In the end, the poem remained, although Wordsworth relegated it to the end of the collection for further editions.

Indeed, the importance of the local West Country landscape to the poems of *Lyrical Ballads* is considerable. Were the 'caverns measureless to man' mentioned in 'Kubla Khan' inspired by nothing more exotic or far-flung than the caves at nearby Cheddar Gorge? It's certainly true that Coleridge blamed his inability to finish the poem on the arrival of an unidentified 'person from Porlock', who, if such a person existed at all and this wasn't just the poet's excuse for 'colygraphia' (that is, writer's block), may have been Coleridge's doctor (and opium dealer) from the nearby Somerset coastal village. So we arguably have the West Country to thank for inspiring 'Kubla Khan' in the first place, and we can also blame the West Country for the fact that it's unfinished.

While they were busy composing some of the most famous poems in the English language, Coleridge and Wordsworth were also fending off rumours that they were not English poets at all but French spies. Partly so they could socialise with Coleridge, the Wordsworths rented the nearby house at Alfoxden. Unfortunately, their night-time walks – armed with notebooks – attracted suspicion from the locals, who were wary of Dorothy Wordsworth's dark complexion and the strange accents of these unfamiliar tourists.

These suspicions led to a Home Office investigator being sent down to Somerset to check out the rumours. The servants attending on the Wordsworths told him that they'd overheard the poets, while at dinner, talking of spies – they recalled that a 'Spy Noza' had specifically been mentioned. In reality, Coleridge and the Wordsworths had been discussing the work of the philosopher Spinoza. The government official returned to London having concluded that the poets were not spies but mere oddballs.

But such a visit put both Wordsworth and Coleridge off remaining in England for much longer. In 1798, the year that *Lyrical Ballads* was published, the poets left Somerset to tour Germany, and so ended perhaps the most fruitful and important period in either of their careers, and one of the most momentous in the history of English literature.

Bath Time

Although it is the city with which she is most closely associated (and the tourist industry in Bath makes much of the association), Jane Austen hated Bath the first time she visited it, and was very glad to escape it.

Austen first visited Bath in 1797 when her aunt and uncle invited her to stay with them in Paragon Buildings in the north of the city. Although none of her letters from this inaugural visit survive, David Nokes has described Austen's first Bath experience, in *The Oxford Guide to Literary Britain and Ireland*, as 'not auspicious'. It can't have helped that it rained for much of the month that she was there. She nevertheless returned several times over the next few years, to stay with her aunt and uncle, the marvellously named Leigh-Perrots. But Austen didn't exactly warm to the city, satirising it in her novel *Northanger Abbey* by having her naïve and easily impressed heroine, Catherine Morland, fall in love with the place. Relieved to return to Steventon when her latest stay was over in 1800, Austen arrived home only for her family to announce that they were moving away . . . to Bath! She did the only thing a young nineteenth-century woman could do in the circumstances. She fainted.

We know surprisingly little about Austen's attitudes to the city with which she is most closely associated. She wrote only five letters while she was in Bath – there are only five that have survived, at least – and these tell us little about how Austen felt about it. We don't know much about what Jane Austen thought of a lot of things. The only time she mentions Wordsworth, for instance, is in *Sanditon*, but since this sole reference to the poet is made by one of Austen's characters, it's difficult to infer from it whether Austen enjoyed *Lyrical Ballads*. As John Mullan has pointed out, even the quotation adorning the English ten-pound note, 'I declare after all there is no enjoyment like reading!', is spoken by a character in one of her novels, *Pride and Prejudice*, and the woman who utters it, Lady Caroline Bingley, shows no interest in books anywhere else in the novel, and is merely trying to impress Mr Darcy with this statement.

As a teenager yet to discover the joys of Bath, Austen wrote a wonderful short parody of the history books of the day. Bath was the place where Macaulay's *History of England* was completed – no, not the one by Thomas Babington Macaulay, but Catharine Macaulay (1731–91), the author of a hugely popular work of history and the first truly popular woman historian writing in English. As Bridget Hill notes in the *Oxford Dictionary of National Biography* entry for Macaulay, 'For a woman to have conceived of such a project in the eighteenth century was extraordinary.' Although the eight-volume project was begun in London, Macaulay wrote the final volumes in Bath, where she was living in Alfred House, on Alfred Street, with her friend the Reverend Thomas Wilson. Wilson had an extensive library, which he allowed Macaulay to use for her research for the *History*.

Thanks to the popularity of her *History of England*, Macaulay had become known as 'the Celebrated Mrs Macaulay' almost overnight, although, somewhat predictably, some of the (invariably male) reviewers preferred to focus on the fact that she was a woman. The *Monthly Review*, for instance, expressed the wish that 'the same degree of genius and application had been exerted in more suitable pursuits', going on to assert that 'though we are persuaded, from the specimen before us, that the fair sex have powers to keep pace with, if not to outstrip us, in the arduous paths of literature; yet we would by no means recommend such a laborious competition to the practice of our lovely countrywomen'.

Macaulay's *History of England* (1763–83) covers much of the seventeenth century from the accession of King James I in 1603 until the crowning of William and Mary in 1689. It won her widespread acclaim. But in 1778 she remarried a man less than half her age, and many of her literary friends shunned her. Some of her supporters had already abandoned her for her enthusiastic endorsement of the Commonwealth under Oliver Cromwell in the fourth volume of the *History*. She suddenly dropped from view and went from enjoying the limelight as a fêted historian to being largely forgotten. Now, she is eclipsed by her namesake, the nineteenth-century historian Thomas Babington Macaulay, whose *History of England* is now far better known than hers.

Mother Hubbard of Yealmpton

The village of Yealmpton (pronounced 'Yampton') is a few miles east of Plymouth. Market Street boasts a house built around 400 years ago with something you don't see every day: a thatched dog on the roof. This is Mother Hubbard's Cottage, and it was supposedly the home of the woman who inspired the nursery rhyme of Old Mother Hubbard.

I say 'supposedly' because it's nearly always impossible to pin down a nursery rhyme's origins in any definite way. According to some of the more fanciful (and, frankly, incredible) theories out there, Humpty Dumpty was originally a cannon in the English Civil War, Doctor Foster who went to Gloucester was really King Edward I, and Cardinal Wolsey seems to have inspired just about every nursery rhyme character from Little Boy Blue to Humpty Dumpty to Mother Hubbard herself – which brings me back to Yealmpton and that cottage.

'Old Mother Hubbard' was one of the most popular publications of the entire nineteenth century, with sales in the tens of thousands within just a few months of publication. Its instant bestseller status may partly have stemmed from the public's belief that it was some sort of political satire, but nobody seems to know what it was satirising. A sequel to the story was published very shortly after. It inspired rival productions, such as 'The Comic Adventures of Old Mother Lantry and Her Wonderful

Goat', and gave its name to a style of dress (a loose-fitting smock) and, in Canada, a kind of duffel coat. It might even be viewed as a precursor to the nonsense verse of later nineteenth-century writers like Edward Lear and Lewis Carroll, given its surreal touches. When Mother Hubbard returns from buying red and white wine for her dog (a detail it's probably best to gloss over), she finds it standing on its head. At other points, it's variously smoking a pipe, dancing a jig, feeding her cat, reading a newspaper, and riding a goat.

Who 'Mother Hubbard' was remains shrouded in mystery. The name first appeared in the late 1570s when Edmund Spenser, the author of *The Faerie Queene*, wrote a satirical poem called 'Mother Hubberd's Tale' – but in Spenser's poem, Mother Hubberd is the narrator rather than the subject of the tale, and she has no connection to bones or cupboards, although a dog is mentioned. The nursery rhyme as we know it came into existence in 1805, and this is where the cottage in Yealmpton enters the story.

The author of the poem, Sarah Catherine Martin (1768– 1826), is a curious character all by herself: she was a vivacious socialite and a lover of Prince William, the future King William IV. (He even proposed to her, but she turned him down.) She came up with 'Old Mother Hubbard' while she was staying with her future brother-in-law, a Tory MP named John Pollexfen Bastard, at Kitley House in Yealmpton. Martin, who had something of a reputation as a chatterbox, had begun to irritate her host while he was trying to write, until he reportedly told her to 'run away and write one of your stupid little rhymes'. (This was probably not the first time, and would definitely not be the last, that a Tory Bastard would be so dismissive of the arts.)

Some have doubted whether Martin herself was the author of the rhyme, though she certainly took the credit for the illustrations which accompanied the 1805 chapbook (a small, usually cheaply produced booklet used to disseminate popular literature). Others have asserted that Martin not only composed the rhyme but took inspiration from the housekeeper at Kitley, who according to local legend lived in the cottage now known in her honour as 'Mother Hubbard's Cottage'. It would appear that she based the rhythm of 'Old Mother Hubbard' on an earlier rhyme, 'Old Dame Trot, and Her Comical Cat', which had been published in 1803 but had been in circulation for nearly a hundred years before that. As Iona and Peter Opie note in *The Oxford Dictionary of Nursery Rhymes*, the similarities between the two rhymes are too close to be considered coincidental:

> Old Dame Trot,
> Some cold fish had got,
> Which for pussy,
> She kept in Store,
> When she looked there was none
> The cold fish had gone,
> For puss had been there before.
>
> She went to the butcher's
> To buy her some meat,
> When she came back
> She lay dead at her feet.

Why Old Dame Trot's cat perished in the mists of nursery-rhyme history while Old Mother Hubbard's dog flourished is difficult to say; as the Opies note, 'Old Dame Trot' is an altogether more modern piece of verse. What's more, the first stanza of Martin's rhyme has a different form and metre from the subsequent poem, so it may be that the first six lines are substantially older than the rest. But it was Martin's surreal rhyme about a talented dog and a bare cupboard that would grip the public imagination.

In Yealmpton you can visit Mother Hubbard's Cottage and find the cupboards anything but bare. Indeed, there's plenty of food on offer: it's now a Chinese takeaway and restaurant.

Strange Omens in Gittisham

Let's travel to the small village of Gittisham, around 12 miles east of Exeter, where Joanna Southcott was raised, shortly after her birth in nearby Taleford in 1750.

Southcott is not widely known now, and for much of her life she seemed destined for a life lived in obscurity. She spent her first forty years working as a servant (a sort of Mother Hubbard figure, if you will) and a dairy maid, and even as an upholsterer, until one day in the early 1790s her life changed. She began to experience a series of visions and soon attracted a following among the locals, who became convinced that she had the gift of prophecy. Between 1801 and 1814, she published a whopping sixty-five books and pamphlets comprising around 5,000 pages in total, each outlining her forebodings and ideas. From a fringe figure in south Devon, she became a national celebrity: it's estimated that at least 108,000 copies of her books were circulated, and by the time of her death she had attracted well over 20,000 followers.

The majority of her devotees were women – attracted, it would appear, by the proto-feminist aspects of some of Southcott's work. Although her writings were often incomprehensible – 'almost illiterate', in the words of one commentator – her prophecies concerning bad harvests and other harbingers of the supposed Second Coming attracted the support of a number of influential adherents.

Then, in 1814, Southcott announced that she was pregnant

(at the improbably late age of sixty-four) with the new Messiah, named Shiloh, whom she would bring into the world on 19 October. When that eagerly awaited day came and no baby arrived, things fizzled out somewhat, and within a couple of months Southcott was dead. Exactly when she died is difficult to say, on account of her numerous followers' determination to hang on to her body until she was spectacularly and somewhat improbably raised from the dead. When this, too, failed to happen, they reluctantly agreed to its burial, though only after it began to decay and putrefy.

At her death, Southcott had left behind a locked wooden box, with express instructions that it was not to be opened until a time of national crisis – and even then, only if twenty-four bishops of the Church of England were present, as if her 'great box' were some latter-day Ark of the Covenant. During both the Crimean War and the Great War, people tried – and failed – to persuade enough bishops to get together to open Southcott's box. The mystery of what was contained within continued.

Then, in Bedford in 1919, a group calling themselves the Panacea Society took up Southcott's ideas, and set about trying to locate and open Southcott's locked box, which had become lost by this time. According to one account, the box was finally opened in 1927, when it was found to contain nothing more than a rusted horse pistol and an old lottery ticket – not a winning one, presumably.

But despite this rather anticlimactic end – both to her life and her legacy – the influence of Joanna Southcott was considerable. In his seminal 1966 book *The Making of the English Working Class*, E. P. Thompson called her England's greatest prophetess. Now, her name is all but forgotten. Prophecy is not what it used to be.

The Riddles of Exeter

Southcott may have been accused of speaking in riddles, her prophecies no more credible than those of Mother Shipton 300 years earlier, but in fact riddles have been part of English literature for almost as long as the word 'English' has been around.

Here's a riddle for you: What hangs down by the thigh of a man, under his cloak, yet is stiff and hard? When the man pulls up his robe, he puts the head of this hanging thing into that familiar hole of matching length which he has filled many times before. Got it? A key, of course! This is one of a number of riddles found in the Exeter Book, one of the jewels in the crown of Anglo-Saxon literature. In 2016, it was recognised by UNESCO as 'the foundation volume of English literature'.

The riddles of the Exeter Book show a surprising aspect of Anglo-Saxon monkish life. For one thing, as with the example above, many of them are shot through with sexual innuendo. Consider this one:

I am a wondrous creature: to women a thing of joyful expectation, to close-lying companions serviceable. I harm no city-dweller excepting my slayer alone. My stem is erect and tall – I stand up in bed – and whiskery somewhere down below. Sometimes a countryman's quite comely daughter will venture, bumptious girl, to get a grip on me. She assaults my red self and seizes my head

and clenches me in a cramped place. She will soon feel
the effect of her encounter with me, this curl-locked
woman who squeezes me. Her eye will be wet.

If your answer to this little riddle is anything other than
'onion', I suggest you take a long hard look at yourself.

What was the point of such riddles? To entertain?
Perhaps, although Craig Williamson has suggested that
they may have been part of a courting ritual and a way of
catching lewd-minded would-be spouses out. If they had
a dirty mind, their thoughts would not turn to onions but
to . . . something else. This theory is appealing, but quite
why the riddles were written, and to what purpose they
were put, we can only guess. What is interesting is that
they were written at all. Before the English language even
had a full translation of the Bible, it had been put to use
to produce such diverting brainteasers as these.

But it's not just its amusing riddles that make the Exeter
Book such a literary treat. The book has had an appreciable
influence on twentieth-century literature, thanks to the
other poems it contains. The Exeter Book is our source for
'The Seafarer', which Ezra Pound translated into modern
English, and it also contains 'The Wanderer', a favourite of
W. H. Auden. In 1914, a young J. R. R. Tolkien read the
following phrase in the book, 'Éala éarendel engla beorhtast
/ ofer middangeard monnum sended' ('Hail Earendel,
brightest of angels / above the middle-earth sent unto men'),
and the word 'middangeard' lodged in his mind, later to
resurface as 'Middle-earth' in the world of *The Lord of the
Rings*. (Middle-earth isn't actually the name of the *world* of
Tolkien's fiction, merely a region of that world, which
is named Arda.)

The Exeter Book is housed in Exeter Cathedral, in one of the finest libraries in all of Britain, and in Exeter city centre there is a sculpture decorated with the Exeter riddles. So as you explore the city, you can see an early part of England's literary heritage literally inscribed on a modern artwork. And, of course, you can try to solve the riddles and find out just how dirty your or your spouse's mind is.

Manderley and Menabilly

Daphne du Maurier, whose archive is located at the University of Exeter, came from a family that had literature in its blood. Her father was the actor Gerald du Maurier, while her grandfather, George du Maurier, was responsible for one of the runaway literary successes of the 1890s, the novel (and hugely popular stage adaptation) *Trilby*, which gave us the name for the hat. Her cousins inspired J. M. Barrie, a friend of the family, to create Peter Pan and the Lost Boys. But now Daphne is surely the most famous du Maurier of them all, with novels which have sold in the millions and inspired some of the most celebrated films of the twentieth century.

Her teenage years were spent at coastal Fowey, which left a profound mark on her and is the setting for two of her novels, *Frenchman's Creek* and *Jamaica Inn*. Her first novel, *The Loving Spirit* (1931), is about Cornish shipbuilders. An army officer named Frederick Browning, impressed by the novel's evocative descriptions of the Cornish coast, set off to see the landscape for himself. Hearing that the author of the novel lived nearby, he extended an invitation to her, and a year later the pair were married (du Maurier proposed to him, having turned down his earlier proposal because she didn't believe in marriage; she then changed her mind).

Daphne du Maurier adored the Cornish landscape. She claimed to love Menabilly, the country estate which she rented and restored, more than she did people. Despite this, her most famous novel, *Rebecca* (1937), was written far away from her beloved Cornwall, while she was living in Alexandria in Egypt with her husband, who was stationed there. Once again, nostalgia for an absent British place – or rather, a British place one is absent from – feeds into one of the most famous novels (and opening lines) of the twentieth century. Manderley, the Cornish house in that novel, is really Menabilly. Daphne also wrote a historical novel about Menabilly, *The King's General* (1946), set during the English Civil War and drawing on real-life events surrounding the house – including the story of the skeleton of a Cavalier soldier (which had been found, somewhat improbably, sitting upright on a stool in a secret room in one of the buttresses).

Of course, the numerous adaptations of du Maurier's work helped to bring her fiction to an even larger audience. Alfred Hitchcock, especially, was a fan, and adapted three of her works – *Jamaica Inn*, 'The Birds', and *Rebecca* – for the big screen. The Nicolas Roeg film *Don't Look Now* (1973) is also based on one of her short stories, as is the 1952 film *My Cousin Rachel*, starring Richard Burton. All of this brought her fame and financial success.

Despite this, in 1969, the same year she became Dame Daphne du Maurier for services to literature, she had to give up Menabilly (when the family who owned it, the Rashleighs, would not renew the lease), and, thereafter, wrote virtually no more fiction. She died in Cornwall, the county that had fired her imagination for so many years and provided the setting for many of her most famous novels and stories, twenty years later.

Round the Table at Tintagel

As we move along the Cornish coast we near the end of our literary peregrinations. Tintagel came to be associated with King Arthur in the Middle Ages and, as with most things, it's all Geoffrey of Monmouth's fault.

The associations between King Arthur and Cornwall are well established. In a book about her beloved county, *Vanishing Cornwall*, Daphne du Maurier wrote that Arthur is to Cornwall what Theseus is to Greece. And it all began with Tintagel, because, according to Geoffrey of Monmouth, Tintagel is where Arthur began. Tintagel was, Geoffrey said, the place where Arthur was conceived.

Contrary to popular belief, Geoffrey never claimed that Arthur was *born* at Tintagel – that would not be suggested until the fifteenth century, when William of Worcester wrote about Tintagel as the king's birthplace and childhood home. What's more, Geoffrey's choice of this remote place in Cornwall as the site of Arthur's conception may have been nothing more than canny political flattery: his patron, Robert, Earl of Gloucester, was the half-brother of Reginald de Dunstanville, who had recently married a Cornish heiress. Tintagel's subsequent role in the Arthurian story, for all that, may have been the result of medieval product placement.

Arthur's court, famously, was at Camelot – although where that was supposed to be has kept historians scratching their heads for centuries. Interestingly, the earliest reference to King Arthur's court, in a Welsh tale called *Culhwch and Olwen*, places it at Celliwig, an unidentified place probably situated somewhere in Cornwall, if only in chroniclers' and poets' imaginations.

Then in 2000, a previously unknown play from around 1500 written in the Cornish language, *Bewnans Ke*, was discovered among the papers of a Welsh scholar. The first part of the play dramatises the acts of the British saint Kea, but the second half focuses on Arthur's scraps with the Romans and with his nephew Mordred. This play also names Celliwig, not Camelot, as the home of Arthur's court. It was only in French romances of the twelfth century that Camelot became Arthur's court. Geoffrey of Monmouth never mentions it.

More intriguing still is the underhand story of how Arthur was conceived. His father, Uther Pendragon, wished to have his way with somebody else's wife – Igraine, wife of Gorlois – so his trusty wizard Merlin used magic to help Uther to assume the likeness of Gorlois so he could go to bed with the beautiful Igraine. And it is on this sleazy act of deception that the tourist industry of Tintagel is founded.

In the 1930s, a custard powder manufacturer bearing the glorious name of F. T. Glasscock built King Arthur's Hall on Fore Street. The building was designed to serve as the headquarters of the Fellowship of the Knights of the Round Table, which Glasscock had founded in 1927. The Fellowship conduct a range of activities including fundraising, visiting libraries to give talks, and hosting garden parties.

We've come all the way to the edge of mainland Britain, so here we must end our literary journey – by returning, in a sense, to the dawn of British literature and the stories of King Arthur. According to some scholars, Arthur made his debut in literature very early on, in a poem from the early seventh century, *Y Gododdin*, written by the Welsh bard Aneirin. The poet praises a warrior, Gwawrddur, but goes on to state that 'he was no Arthur'. And it is with this rather muted praise for poor Gwawrddur's talents that we end our bookish journey through Britain – back at the beginnings of Britain's literary history, at the end of a literary tour that has taken us from Jan de Groot's octagonal table at John O'Groats to King Arthur's Round Table in Cornwall.

Further down the Cornish coast from Tintagel we find Land's End. When the pioneering travel writer Celia Fiennes reached this point in the late seventeenth century, she 'clamber'd over [the rocks] as farre as safety permitted me' but contented herself with looking out to sea, for she 'was not willing to venture . . . into a Forreign Kingdom'. The idea of crossing the vast expanse of ocean and setting foot on new shores, a land with its own literary heritage, is appealing. Shortly before Fiennes made her journey to Land's End, a woman named Anne Bradstreet, who had crossed the Atlantic to begin a new life in America, became the first published poet of the New World. Her book of poems marked the starting point of another nation's bookish history . . . but then that's a book for, well, for another book.

Acknowledgements

I would like to thank the following people for their help with this book: my parents, without whom it's fair to say I wouldn't have been able to write it; Rachel Adcock, for valuable suggestions and conversations; Mark Richards, Becky Walsh, Caroline Westmore and all the wonderful team at John Murray; Chris Wellbelove, for judicious advice; my copy-editor, Hilary Hammond; and Nosy Cat, without whose never-failing encouragement (to borrow from and adapt P. G. Wodehouse) this book would have been finished much sooner.

Select Bibliography

Daiches, David, and John Flower, *Literary Landscapes of the British Isles: A Narrative Atlas* (Bell & Hyman, 1979)

Evans, Jeremy, *Classic Literary Walks* (Oxford Illustrated Press, 1990)

Hahn, Daniel, *The Oxford Guide to Literary Britain and Ireland*, edited by Nicholas Robins (Oxford University Press, 2008)

Holloway, John (ed.), *The Oxford Book of Local Verses* (Oxford University Press, 1987)

Kelly, Stuart, *Scott-Land: The Man Who Invented a Nation* (Polygon, 2011)

Kemp, David, *The Pleasures and Treasures of Britain: A Discerning Traveller's Companion* (Dundurn Press, 1992)

Meredith, Don, *Where the Tigers Were: Travels through Literary Landscapes* (University of South Carolina Press, 2001)

Millar, Eloise, and Sam Jordison, *Literary London* (Michael O'Mara, 2016)

Parsons, Nicholas T., *The Joy of Bad Verse* (Collins, 1988)

Williamson, Craig (ed.), *A Feast of Creatures: Anglo-Saxon Riddle-Songs* (University of Pennsylvania Press, 2011)

Index

INDEX

Thackeray, William
Makepeace, 136
thesaurus: meaning, 52
Thomas, David John
('Jack'), 164
Thomas, Dylan, 164–5
Thomas, Edward: visits
Dunwich, 116;
'Adlestrop', 171–3
Thomson, James, 89
*Three Weeks in Wet Sheets: A
Moist Visitor to Malvern*,
168
Tintagel, Cornwall, 218
Todd, Sweeney, 123
Tolkien, Edith, 199–200
Tolkien, J. R. R.: and
'middle earth', 23; influ-
enced by J. W. Dunne,
43; in Inklings, 81; eccen-
tricities, 82–3; in
Bournemouth, 199–200;
reads *The Exeter Book*, 214;
The Lord of the Rings, 199,
214; *The Silmarillion*, 200
Treacle Mine Road,
Wincanton, 85
Turing, Alan, 91
Turner, J. M. W., 178, 180
Tussaud, Madame, 123
Tusser, Thomas: death,
119; *Hundredth Good
Pointes of Husbandrie*, 117
Twain, Mark, 64
Tynan, Kenneth, 46

Uniformity, Act of (1564),
75
Uther Pendragon, 180, 219
Uttoxeter, 61–2

Vanity of Vanities (1660
poem), 6
Veigel, Eva Marie, 130
Victoria, Queen:
McGonagall requests
patronage, 7; praises
Marie Corelli, 78
Vyver, Bertha, 79

Wakefield: and Robin
Hood, 63

Walpole, Horace, 96, 98;
The Castle of Otranto, 175,
178
Walpole, Robert, 89
'Wanderer, The' (poem),
214
Warwickshire, 74, 75
Watchet, Somerset, 202
Watkins, Gwen, 91
Watkins, Vernon, 91
Waugh, Evelyn, 162–3
Webster, John, 77
Wellington, Arthur
Wellesley, 1st Duke of,
127
Wells, H. G.: Virginia
Woolf disparages, 59;
mocks Henry James, 100;
cricketing, 141
Wesker, Arnold, 161
Wessex: Hardy and Barnes
on, 193–4
Wessex, Earl of: title,
194–5
Wessex, Sophie, Countess
of (*née* Rhys-Jones),
195
West, Richard, 96–7
Westminster Abbey: Poets'
Corner, 129–30, 197
Wharton, Edith, 100–1
Whitby: Abbey, 23, 26;
Cædmon at, 23; as inspir-
ation for *Dracula*, 25–6
White, Gilbert: *Garden
Kalendar*, 184; *The
Natural History and
Antiquities of Selborne*,
183–4
Wight, Isle of, 191
Wilde, Oscar: patronises
Hatchard's, 127; trial
(1895), 159
Wilkinson, Patrick: 'The
Other Side', 91
William IV, King, 208
William, Prince, Duke of
Cambridge, 195
William of Worcester,
218
Williamson, Craig, 214
Wilson, Sir Angus, 91

Wilson, Revd Thomas, 205
Wincanton, Somerset, 85
Winchester, 186–8
Witley, Surrey, 144
Wodehouse, P. G.: golfing
stories, 12; cricketing,
141
Wolsey, Cardinal Thomas,
31, 33
women: in McCullough's
novel, 12
Woof, Robert, 201
Woolf, Virginia, 29; dispar-
ages Arnold Bennett, and
H. G. Wells, 59–60;
testifies at trial of *The
Well of Loneliness*, 139;
Jacob's Room, 59; 'Modern
Novels', 59; *Mrs
Dalloway*, 135–6; *Orlando*,
139
Wordsworth, Dorothy,
39–41, 203
Wordsworth, William:
James Hogg parodies, 15;
born in Cockermouth,
39–40; poem on daffodils,
39–41; and Chatterton,
175–6; and Lake District,
201; meets Coleridge in
Bristol, 201; and
Coleridge's *Ancient
Mariner*, 202; in
Somerset, 202–3;
suspected of being French
spy, 203; 'Lines Written a
Few Miles above Tintern
Abbey', 174; *Lyrical
Ballads* (with Coleridge),
202–3, 205

x (letter): as symbol for
kiss, 184–5

Yealmpton, Devon, 207–8,
210
York, 31, 34–5

Zaleski, Philip and Carol:
*The Fellowship: The
Literary Lives of the
Inklings*, 83

230